# Current Practice in Company Accounts

Frederick Bailey
Senior Lecturer in
Management Sciences
University of Manchester

Accountancy Age Books

Accountancy Age Books
Published by:
Haymarket Publishing Limited
Gillow House
5 Winsley Street
London W1A 2HG
First Published 1973
© Haymarket Publishing Limited
SBN 0 900442 44 1

Printed in Great Britain by
A Wheaton and Company
143 Fore Street
Exeter EX4 3AP
Devon

# Contents

# 7 Company Law                                 103

# 8 Interpretation of Accounts            119

# 9 Ratio Analysis                              135

# 10 Review and Appraisal                   157

# Preface

Nearly all of the literature on financial accounting falls into one of two categories between which there is a great intellectual gulf. On the one hand are books which set out the currently accepted rules of professional practice, often in great detail but in an uncritical manner and without any historical perspective. At the other extreme stand some academic contributions, written from a position outside the accounting profession, which set out to ridicule the inconsistencies and lack of intellectual foundations of financial accounting practice, and to build a new framework of financial reporting on foundations of their own choosing.

This book is an important contribution to bridging the gulf between these two viewpoints. The author sees the need to know the rules of current practice and he shows real sympathy for the practical problems of accountants; but he approaches his subject critically and with a clear sense of standing at one point in a process of continuing development. The legal requirements relating to company accounts are set out here, as are the highly influential requirements and recommendations of the Stock Exchange and the professional accounting bodies. But the reader is encouraged at every stage to think about the objectives and problems involved as well as the rule book as it stands today.

Thus this book furthers the purposes of the series in which it is published—to present academic thinking on accounting problems in a form that will be useful to practitioners and to students; to contribute to and raise the intellectual standard of the discussion of current issues and controversies relating to accounting principles and procedures; and to reduce the dependence of British readers upon American literature written in the context of a legal and commercial environment that is not fully applicable in Britain.

This volume is also appearing at a particularly appropriate time. It approaches its theme in the same enquiring spirit which it seems that accounting students will be expected to adopt during part at least of their education and training under the new arrangements which the professional bodies are now introducing.

Department of Accounting University of Kent

PETER BIRD

# Introduction

There is considerable discussion and criticism of financial accounts
published by companies at the present time. A number of cases have
illustrated forcefully the weaknesses of the traditional statements. In
particular the takeover of AEI by GEC, during which a forecast
profit of £10 million became an actual loss of £4.5 million (a difference
which was dismissed by some commentators as an unimportant 'paper
adjustment') demonstrated the amount of estimation which enters
into the profit calculation.

Published accounts are reports of past history, but they deal
with continuing operations. Judgement is involved in preparing
accounts because it is necessary to use estimates of the future outcome
of events. Accounting conventions and the law constrain the content
and form of the reports but leave room for directors to choose methods
which they believe represent best the financial affairs of the company.
This text is an attempt to explain the foundation on which published
accounts are built, to describe the information which may be found
in them, to indicate some of the ways in which the statements may be
used and to draw attention to the main problems which will be
encountered in using them, in the context of the United Kingdom.

Changes are being made and will continue to be made in the
details which companies have to publish. Professional accountants,

through the Accounting Standards Steering Committee, are actively pursuing a policy of reform. The entry of Britain into the European Community will almost certainly mean changes in company law. There is no suggestion, however, that the basis of accounting statements is likely to be changed quickly—except, possibly, for the introduction of statements adjusted for price level changes, as an addition to the historic cost accounts.

The Jenkins Committee on Company Law suggested that the function of accounts is not fully appreciated by many who attempt to use them. If this small volume helps to increase understanding it will serve its purpose.

# 1 The Accounting Framework

*'To my accounts . . . and was at it till past twelve at night,
it being bitter cold: but yet I was well satisfied with my worke . . .
I have laid up above 500 l this year above what I was worth this day
twelve month.'*[1]

### 1.1 The Structure of Accounts

Every limited company publishes annually a report to its members
containing a balance sheet and profit and loss account (the accounts
of the company), the auditors' report on the accounts and the
directors' report on the state of affairs of the company. The annual
report frequently contains a copy of the chairman's statement,
summaries of financial information for several years and occasionally,
but with increasing frequency, a flow of funds statement. This latter
statement appears in various forms with different titles, such as cash
flow statement, 'where got, where gone' statement. This book is
concerned mainly with the three formal accounting statements, the
balance sheet, profit and loss account and flow of funds statement and
the first stage is to describe the structure of these accounts.

It is not easy to describe the nature of accounting statements
precisely in a few words. They may be regarded as collections of
statistics about the financial affairs of an organization, put together
according to a customary pattern. The main plan or framework is

1. PEPYS, SAMUEL. Diary. 31 December 1664.

1

readily recognisable but the details may vary according to the
judgement of the person who prepares the statement. The basis of the
accounts is an analysis of the financial effects of transactions entered
into by the company, including the rights, benefits and obligations
arising from those transactions. The position described is that of the
company as an entity (or of a group of companies regarded as a single
entity) in its relations with others such as shareholders, employees,
customers and suppliers.

### 1.2 Cash Flow and Flow of Funds

The main structure of the accounts may be demonstrated by means
of an example, setting out a number of transactions in a variety of

### Example 1

RECEIPTS AND PAYMENTS FOR THE YEAR ENDED 31 DECEMBER 19. . .

| Cash Received | (£) | (£) |
|---|---:|---:|
| Issue of shares | | 6,000 |
| Sale of goods | 20,000 | |
| Less amount owing by customers (debtors) | 2,000 | 18,000 |
| | | 24,000 |
| Cash Paid | | |
| Purchase of goods: | | |
| subsequently sold | 15,000 | |
| still held in stock | 4,000 | |
| | 19,000 | |
| Less amount owing to suppliers (creditors) | 3,000 | 16,000 |
| Plant purchased and paid for | | 5,000 |
| Expenses paid | | 2,000 |
| | | 23,000 |
| Cash in hand | | 1,000 |
| | | 24,000 |

ways. Consider the transactions in Example 1 which are recorded so as to show their effect on the cash position of the company. An action does not necessarily cause an immediate change in the cash position—goods are sold for £20,000 but the receipt of cash is deferred for the period of credit allowed to the customer. In the illustration the full history of each receipt and payment is given commencing with the recognition of a transaction to be recorded in the accounting system.

*Example 2*

| Sources of Funds | (£) |
|---|---|
| Issue of shares | 6,000 |
| Sale of goods | 20,000 |
| Credit given by suppliers (creditors) | 3,000 |
| | 29,000 |

| Uses of Funds | |
|---|---|
| Credit allowed to customers (debtors) | 2,000 |
| Purchase of goods—subsequently sold | 15,000 |
| —held in stock | 4,000 |
| Plant purchased | 5,000 |
| Expenses | 2,000 |
| Cash in hand | 1,000 |
| | 29,000 |

If the items are rearranged, so as to separate the transactions which are combined in the calculation of receipts and payments the basic structure of the flow of funds statement emerges as shown in Example 2 which contains the same figures as Example 1. Although this is only a slight rearrangement of the data in the cash statement, there is a considerable change in the viewpoint. Essentially this is a record of transactions entered into by the company rather than the cash flows generated by those transactions. On the other hand, because the giving and receiving of credit is accounted for, the residual change in cash position is automatically incorporated as the difference between the sources and the uses of funds.

Two classes of item are recognized in this statement:

1.   *Items which record changes in assets and obligations of the company.* The issue of shares for £6,000 was originally recorded in the books of account from two aspects:

> *Source of Funds*
> Issue of shares                                    £6,000
>
> *Use of Funds*
> Increase in cash in hand                           £6,000

The aspect recorded as an issue of shares represents the obligation of the company: the increase in the claims of shareholders on the company. The change in cash, representing the acquisition of an asset, has been subsequently modified by other transactions and only the net increase in cash of £1,000 during the period is stated in the flow of funds statement.

2.   *Items which do not record changes in assets and obligations.* These are usually operating or trading transactions such as sales and expenses. For example the record of expenses paid is as follows:

> *Source of Funds*
> Decrease in cash in hand                           £2,000

This is one of the items, referred to in (1) above, which is deducted from the £6,000 increase in cash produced by the issue of shares to reduce the net increase in cash to £1,000.

> *Use of Funds*
> Expenses paid                                      £2,000

The aspect recorded under 'Use of Funds' does not represent a change in an asset or obligation of the company although it explains why the cash in hand has decreased. The change in cash is recorded separately.

If the operating or trading items are merged into a single item the usual form of the flow of funds statement emerges as shown in Example 3.

*Example 3*

| Items to be grouped together: | (£) | (£) |
|---|---|---|
| Sale of goods | | 20,000 |
| Cost of goods sold | 15,000 | |
| Expenses | 2,000 | 17,000 |
| | | |
| Funds from operations (cash flow) | | 3,000 |

FLOW OF FUNDS STATEMENT FOR THE YEAR ENDED 31 DECEMBER 19 . . .

| *Sources of Funds* | (£) |
|---|---|
| Issue of shares | 6,000 |
| Funds from operations (see above) | 3,000 |
| Credit given by suppliers (creditors) | 3,000 |
| | |
| | 12,000 |

| *Uses of Funds* | |
|---|---|
| Credit allowed to customers (debtors) | 2,000 |
| Purchase of goods for stock | 4,000 |
| Plant purchased | 5,000 |
| Cash in hand | 1,000 |
| | |
| | 12,000 |

*1.3 The Balance Sheet and Profit and Loss Account*
A comparison of this statement with a balance sheet suggests that they are closely related. The balance sheet may be described as a statement of the assets of an organisation and the claims upon the organisation. The flow of funds statement records changes in assets and claims arising from transactions. The items which are grouped together to

derive the funds from operations are those normally appearing in the profit and loss account. If this were a record of the first year of the company's life there is only one step needed to convert the statements into a balance sheet and profit and loss acount. Because there were no assets and claims at the beginning the amounts recorded in the flow of funds statement represent assets and claims existing at the end of the year as well as changes during the year. If the values are adjusted according to recognised conventions the result of this valuation adjustment will be a balance sheet and profit and loss acount. For example plant has a limited economic life and will be reduced in value by writing off depreciation as an expense over that life. If the plant has an estimated life of ten years £500 might be written off in this year. The result, with slight rearrangement and classification of the items, might appear as in Example 4.

*Example 4*

PROFIT AND LOSS ACCOUNT FOR THE YEAR ENDED 31 DECEMBER 19 . . .

|  | (£) | (£) |
|---|---|---|
| Sales |  | 20,000 |
| Cost of goods sold | 15,000 |  |
| Expenses | 2,000 |  |
| Depreciation | 500 | 17,500 |
| Net profit for the year |  | 2,500 |

BALANCE SHEET AS AT 31 DECEMBER 19 . . .

|  | (£) | (£) |
|---|---|---|
| *Share Capital and Reserves* |  |  |
| Issued share capital |  | 6,000 |
| Reserves—undistributed profit |  | 2,500 |
|  |  | 8,500 |
| *Current Liabilities*—creditors |  | 3,000 |
|  |  | 11,500 |

*Fixed Assets*

| | | |
|---|---|---|
| Plant at cost | 5,000 | |
| Less depreciation | 500 | 4,500 |

*Current Assets*

| | | |
|---|---|---|
| Stock | 4,000 | |
| Debtors | 2,000 | |
| Cash | 1,000 | 7,000 |
| | | 11,500 |

If the flow of funds statement records a later year in the life of the company then all items in that statement, including creditors, debtors and cash represents changes during the year. The changes in assets and claims must be related to the position at the beginning of the year in order to produce the balance sheet at the end of the year. Example 5 illustrates this by introducing a balance sheet at the beginning of the year. The column headed change is identical to the balance sheet in the last illustration. The third column combines the opening position and the changes during the year to show the position at the end of the period.

*Example 5*

BALANCE SHEET

| | | 1st Jan | | Change | | 31st Dec |
|---|---|---|---|---|---|---|
| *Capital* | (£) | (£) | (£) | (£) | (£) | (£) |
| Issued shares | | 10,000 | | 6,000 | | 16,000 |
| Reserves | | 1,000 | | 2,500 | | 3,500 |
| | | 11,000 | | 8,500 | | 19,500 |
| *Current* | | | | | | |
| *Liabilities* | | 4,000 | | 3,000 | | 7,000 |
| | | 15,000 | | 11,500 | | 26,500 |

*Fixed Assets*

| | | | | | | |
|---|---|---|---|---|---|---|
| Plant at cost | 6,000 | | 5,000 | | 11,000 | |
| Less | | | | | | |
| deprcn | 2,000 | 4,000 | 500 | 4,500 | 2,500 | 8,500 |

*Current Assets*

| | | | | | | |
|---|---|---|---|---|---|---|
| Stock | 7,000 | | 4,000 | | 11,000 | |
| Debtors | 2,000 | | 2,000 | | 4,000 | |
| Cash | 2,000 | 11,000 | 1,000 | 7,000 | 3,000 | 18,000 |
| | | 15,000 | | 11,500 | | 26,500 |

The common factors in the statements which have been illustrated are financial aspects of transactions entered into by the company, such as purchase and sale of goods, giving of credit, receipt and payment of cash, issue of shares and so on. Each transaction may be regarded from two aspects, both of which are recorded in the books of account in the double entry system of book-keeping. A cash sale is recorded as a sale of goods and as a receipt of cash. The payment of a creditor is recorded as a payment of cash and as a reduction in the amount owing. The simplest summary of the transactions is contained in the flow of funds statement which accounts for the financial events which occur during a specified period of time. A more elaborate summary of the same transactions is contained in the profit and loss account and the balance sheet. The balance sheet states those aspects of transactions which represent assets or obligations of the company at the stated date whereas the profit and loss account contains those aspects which represent operating or trading activities, profits and losses. The net profit or loss represents an increase or reduction in the claims of the shareholders and is therefore shown in the balance sheet. The difference between net profit and flow of funds from operations (or cash flow) is caused by valuation adjustments such as depreciation which do not arise from transactions. The 'cash flow' may be regarded in most cases as net profit plus depreciation.

*1.4 The Balance Sheet—Another Viewpoint*

Having examined the way in which the financial accounts are

constructed from the transaction data it is worthwhile looking at the balance sheet and profit and loss account from a different aspect.

The balance sheet of an entity, whether a company or a group of companies, may be described as a list of assets and a list of claims on those assets at a stated date. The two lists have the same sum because claims include not only liabilities of fixed amount such as trade creditors, but also the residual claims of 'owners' or equity shareholders. In a company having a share capital the residual claim is normally represented by the ordinary share capital and reserves, the latter being, in effect, the balancing figure. A rough explanation of the balance sheet would be as follows: if a company realised the assets at the values stated on the balance sheet and paid out claims then the ordinary shareholders would receive the sum of the ordinary share capital plus reserves. If however the assets realised more or less than book values then the difference would be added to or deducted from reserves and hence adjusted on the ordinary shareholders claim. Only if the shareholders claim is reduced to zero are other claims affected by the shortage of assets. This is a rough approximation. A balance sheet is normally drawn up on the basis that the company is a 'going concern', that is it will continue in business for an indefinite period of time. In the event of winding up, other claims may be made which are not recorded in the balance sheet.

In the following discussion it is convenient to define 'net assets' as total assets less fixed claims; thus net assets are equal to equity capital, which is the sum of the ordinary share capital and reserves. The profit and loss account forms a link between the balance sheets at two points of time. It explains the main reason for the continuous change in net assets and reserves by accounting for the profit or loss from operations of the company. Revenues give rise to increases in net assets, expenses represent decreases; a surplus of revenue over expense is a profit which increases the claims of equity and which is recorded as an increase in reserves.

The relationship between the balance sheet and the profit and loss account may be illustrated diagrammatically (see Figure 1.1). At the beginning of a period the balance sheet will show net assets equal to equity. In the terminology of the flow of funds statement the equity is the source of funds used to provide the assets. At the end of the

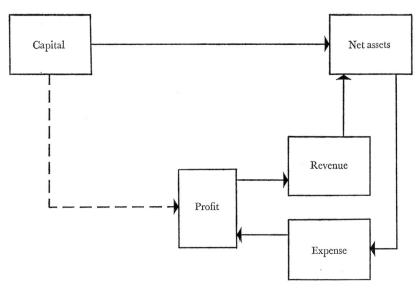

*Figure 1.1    The Structure of the Balance Sheet.*

period the net assets will have changed. Changes in the book value of the net assets will be accounted for in three ways:

1.    *Payment by shareholders for shares issued to them.* The amount will be recorded as an increase in capital that is: the equity will automatically reflect the increase in net assets.

2.    *Profits or losses from operations.* Revenues are earned from sale of goods and services resulting in the acquisition of debtors and cash. Expenses are incurred—the cost of the goods sold, wages and salaries and so on—causing a reduction in net assets. Revenues and expenses are matched in the profit and loss account to calculate profit or loss. If revenues exceed expenses there is an increase in net assets equivalent to the profit earned. This profit is attributed to the equity shareholders and is added to reserves, bringing the balance sheet into balance. The enlarged equity equals the enlarged net assets. Dividends to shareholders are normally recorded in the profit and loss account (technically in the final section of that account dealing with appropriation of profits) so that the surplus added to

reserves represents retained or undistributed profits. The profit
and loss account is therefore an explanation of the change in
net assets and reserves arising from the operations and dividend
payments of the company.

3    *Other profits and losses may by-pass the profit and loss account and be
     adjusted directly in the reserves.* If the directors decided to increase
     the book value of property owned by the company to current
     market value the surplus arising on the revaluation would
     be added to reserves. If the proposed statement of standard
     practice referred to in section 6.3 is adopted the items which
     by-pass the profit and loss acount will be restricted to unrealised
     surpluses on revaluation of fixed assets.

*1.5 Balance Sheet Terminology and Classification*
The balance sheet is more than a list of assets and claims. It is an
attempt to display the information obtained from the records of the
company in a way which reveals the financial position. To this end
the contents are classified by type such as land and buildings, stock
in trade, loans, trade creditors and also placed in appropriate groups.
The groups are not very precisely defined and in some cases there is
room for difference of opinion as to the appropriate grouping. Assets
are grouped into fixed assets, current assets and groups which comprise
both; claims are usually divided into shareholders interests, long term
liabilities and short term or current liabilities.

     *Fixed assets* are those which are held by the company for use in
the business or as long term investments and not for the purpose
of resale in the normal course of trade. They normally comprise assets
with fairly long lives, such as land, buildings, plant and machinery
and vehicles, but the purpose for which they are held rather than the
nature of the asset determines its classification. Television sets held by
a rental company are fixed assets; those held by a retailer for resale
are current assets.

     *Current assets* are stocks of consumable materials or goods for
resale, work in progress, trade debtors, temporary investments and
cash. The main characteristic is that of being continually turned over
in the normal course of trade. They are the assets in which the company
trades and its liquid or near cash assets. In most cases the life of the

asset in the company is short compared with that of fixed assets, but this is not essential. Maturing stocks of whiskey are current assets but may have a longer life than some fixed assets. Current assets are usually listed in order of liquidity, or nearness to realisation in cash.

*Other groups of assets.* The main classification of fixed and current may be modified when a different classification is more informative. The most common change is the grouping together of all investments in subsidiary companies (a subsidiary company may be broadly defined as a company which is controlled by the company the accounts of which are being considered). The Companies Acts require that 'the aggregate amount of assets consisting of shares in, or amounts owing (whether on account of loan or otherwise) from, the company's subsidiaries, distinguishing shares from indebtedness, shall be set out in the balance sheet separately from all the other assets of the company, . . .'[2] This group contains both fixed assets and current assets. There may also be found, included with the assets in some balance sheets, items of expenditure which have not yet been written off as expenses although they do not represent any asset in the normal sense. These include the expenses of formation of the company, expenses of issuing shares and debentures and discount on shares and debentures issued at less than nominal value.

Claims on the company are of many different types ranging from claims of trade creditors falling due for payment within a few days or weeks, through long term loans with fixed maturity dates and terms of repayment, loans convertible into shares, to equity shares with rights to the residue of profit and assets.

*Current liabilities* are grouped together and distinguished from *long term liabilities.* Current liabilities are short term liabilities comprising such items as trade creditors, bank overdrafts, current taxation and proposed dividends. It is often suggested that they consist of liabilities which fall due for payment within 12 months of the balance sheet date, but this is a rough guide line rather than a precise definition. The Institute of Chartered Accountants recommends that corporation tax on the profits for the period covered by the accounts should be disclosed either as an item of current liabilities or as a separate liability

2. Companies Act 1967, Sch. 2, para. 15(2).

with the due date for payment shown.[3] This could include tax due for payment up to nearly 21 months after the balance sheet date. In practice some companies do include all tax on current profits in current liabilities; others separate tax due more than 12 months later. Bank overdrafts are technically repayable at short notice but may represent fairly permanent borrowing. In either case they will be classified as current liabilities. Long term loans nearing maturity which fall due for repayment within 12 months will not normally be reclassified as current liabilities in the United Kingdom. In the case of loans the Companies Acts adopt a different classification distinguishing:

(a)    Bank loans and overdrafts.
(b)    Other loans which are repayable more than 5 years after the balance sheet date (or if repayable by instalments, if any instalments fall due after 5 years).[4]
(c)    By implication, other loans, that is, those due for repayment wholly within 5 years.

*Share capital and reserves* will normally be grouped together, representing the shareholders' interest in the company. Shares may be issued in several classes, some with preferential rights to dividend and possibly to preference in repayment of capital on winding up.

*Issued share capital* is the nominal amount or face value of the shares taken up by members of the company. All shares of the same class will have the same nominal amount and will have equal rights to dividend and to payment when the company is wound up. If the full nominal amount has not been paid to the company, only the amount actually paid will be shown as issued capital—the obligation of the shareholders to pay when called upon to do so will appear from the description of the share capital as partly paid. A company may have converted fully paid shares into stock in which case the balance sheet will show capital stock instead of share capital. There is no material difference between shares and stock.

3. INSTITUTE OF CHARTERED ACCOUNTANTS IN ENGLAND AND WALES,
    Recommendations on Accounting Principles, N27, para 27.
4. Companies Act 1967, Sch. 2, para 8 (1) (d).

*Reserves* consist of three main categories:

1.    Share premium account which arises when shares are issued at
a price in excess of their nominal value. Only the nominal value
(which determines the rights of the holders as between
themselves) is recorded in the share capital, the balance being
recorded separately as premium on shares and classified as a
reserve. The share capital together with the share premium
account represents permanent capital of the company which
cannot be returned to shareholders except on winding up or in
special circumstances usually involving the approval of the
Court.

One occasionally finds a *capital redemption reserve fund* which is
similar in nature. It is possible for a company to issue preference
shares which may be redeemed, either out of the proceeds of a new
issue of shares, or from funds provided by retained profits. The
redemption does not reduce the permanent capital, because if
new shares of equivalent amount are not issued, then a transfer
must be made from the 'free' reserves mentioned in paragraphs
2 and 3 below, to capital redemption reserve. This is treated
as if it were paid up share capital in that it cannot be paid out
to shareholders, although it may be converted into shares by
issuing bonus shares.

2.    Profits realised by the company and not distributed. These
may appear under the heading of profit and loss account,
general reserve or reserves for specified purposes. The division
of retained profits into several categories has little significance
and they may be treated as one amount.

3.    Surpluses arising when the balance sheet value of an asset
exceeds the expenditure incurred on the asset i.e. when the
value has been written up above its cost. The increase in the
asset value creates a matching reserve.

Whilst realised profits represent an amount which can be
distributed to shareholders, such unrealised surpluses may or may not
be distributable. The question is not often a material one because
retained profits tend to be tied up permanently by the growth of the

company and the question of distributing more than a small part does not arise.

The term reserves is used in a technical sense and should not be confused with the common use of the word to denote a surplus of funds or other assets which can be used in an emergency. Reserves are part of the shareholders claim on the company; the assets of the company are recorded elsewhere in the balance sheet.

### 1.6 Valuation of Assets and Liabilities

The contents of the balance sheet and the profit and loss account depend on the recognition and valuation of assets and liabilities. Alternatively, the net assets disclosed by a company depend on the rules for measuring profit, for profit implies an increase in net assets. One can find three methods of arriving at the amounts stated in the balance sheet:

1.    *Nominal or face value* in the case of cash, debtors, capital and liabilities.

2.    *Cost.* Expenditure or residue of expenditure, the benefit of which has not been exhausted at the date of the balance sheet. (In most cases the benefit is identified with a tangible asset such as stock in trade or plant, but it may be, for example, the right to occupy premises represented by the payment of rent in advance or expenditure on research which is expected to benefit future periods.)

3.    *Valuation.* The main examples are:

    (a)  the reduction of current assets (for example, stock and debtors) to realisable value if that is less than cost or face value.

    (b)  the revaluation of fixed assets such as land and buildings and plant and machinery to bring them into line with current prices.

The basis of the figures is found in a number of concepts which can be described rather than defined.

1.    Records of transactions. The accounts comprise a summary of transactions recorded by the company and appropriately

classified. One factor is dominant in the identification of the transaction to be recorded; the passing of title to money or goods or the receipt of services, creating an obligation to pay for them. The receipt of a loan entails the recording of the increase in cash and of the obligation to repay. The receipt and acceptance of goods involves the recording of the liability to the supplier. The double entry system of book-keeping ensures that both aspects of each transaction are recorded. On the other hand a contract in which performance on both sides is to take place in the future will not be recorded. A contract for future delivery of goods is not shown in the balance sheet; the obligation to take delivery and pay for them in due course is assumed to be offset by the value of the goods and neither liability nor asset is revealed. (Provision may be made for an expected loss on the contract but not the full liability unless the goods are worthless.) As the record of an asset is the record of its acquisition the basis of asset valuation is appropriately described as 'historic cost'.

2.     Profit is calculated by matching revenue and expense and this, in turn, influences the amounts stated in the balance sheet. The measurement of profit is influenced by two rules:

(*i*) *The realisation rule.* Revenue is not recognised until it is realised. Realisation is interpreted primarily as a transaction of sale, in which the title to goods passes or services are completed, for a consideration, the monetary value of which can be readily ascertained. This will usually be in the form of cash or indebtedness and the amount received or receivable will be recorded as an asset in the accounts. In the event of the consideration being such that the realisable value is not readily assessable with reasonable certainty, for example, where the transaction is one of barter rather than a sale for a cash consideration—the cost of the goods delivered to the customer may be regarded as the cost of the goods, rights or services received in exchange. The transaction is regarded as a purchase rather than a sale with the effect that no profit is recorded. This interpretation is one illustration of the concept of 'prudence' or 'conservatism' applied to asset valuation.

(*ii*) *The cost matching rule*. Expenditure should be identified with revenue in some systematic way so that revenue and the expense of earning that revenue are recorded in the profit and loss account for the same period. For example, the cost of goods sold must be charged to the profit and loss account for the period in which the revenue from the sale of goods is recognised. In many cases there is no direct connection between revenue and expense and other guides are needed to identify expense. These may be found in a number of conventions:

(a) The value of an asset is based on the expenditure incurred in acquiring it but expenditure is not treated as an asset unless there is a benefit remaining at the end of the period. Any expenditure not classified as an asset or identified with the reduction of a claim automatically becomes an expense. Many expenses are identified with the time periods during which the benefits accrue, rather than directly with revenue earning transactions. For example, rent payable for a period up to the date of the balance sheet is an expense, rent paid in advance for a later period is an asset. 'Expenditure' refers to the transaction incurring the obligation to pay rather than actual payment. If a transaction has not been identified and if payment has not been made at the date of the balance sheet, the decision as to whether an item should be charged to profit and loss account in the period may determine whether it appears as a liability or not. Proposed dividends are recorded in the profit and loss account and so appear in the balance sheet as current liabilities, although there is no legal liability at that date and it is conceivable that the payment, which depends on the decision of the members in general meeting, may not be made.

(b) The cost of assets of limited life should be written off as expense over the period of that life—thus depreciation of plant is an apportionment of the cost to expense in instalments over the useful life of the asset.

(c) Losses which are regarded as inevitable are written off against profits or reserves.

(d) When the outcome is uncertain the record should err on the side of prudent or conservative valuation of net assets. If a range of values is possible a low asset value or a high liability amount is preferred .The reduction of current assets to realisable value has already been referred to. Other examples are the tendency to treat expenditure on research as an expense rather than show an asset of highly uncertain value in the balance sheet and the estimation of liabilities when necessary, to ensure that all expenses and losses incurred up to the date of the balance sheet are taken into account. The term 'provision' used in the accounts includes 'any known liability of which the amount cannot be determined with substantial accuracy'.[5]

3. The valuation and profit measurement rules are interpreted on the assumption that the company is a going concern, that it will continue to operate and not be wound up. Liabilities and losses which might arise only in the event of forced sale or winding up are not taken into account. Thus, the stating of current assets at realisable value which is lower than cost implies realisation in the normal course of business and not in the process of a forced sale. The book value of fixed assets may bear no relationship to realisable value.

4. The concepts on which accounting statements are based are not sufficiently well defined to lead to a unique method of dealing with each transaction. There is often a variety of methods which can be used to value assets or calculate profits and personal judgement plays a large part in deciding which method to adopt. It is generally accepted that a company must be consistent in its choice of method from one period to the next. If one method of stock valuation is adopted at the beginning of a year the same method must be used at the end. This does not prevent change of method but it assumes that change will be infrequent and that if change is made that full disclosure of the effects of the change will be reported.

The 'Fundamental accounting concepts' have been defined in the Statement of Accounting Practice No. 2 issued by the Accounting

5. Companies Act 1967, Sch 2, para 27.

Standards Steering Committee and approved by the major accountancy bodies in Great Britain and Ireland. Paragraph 14 of that statement reads as follows:

> '*Fundamental accounting concepts* are the broad basic assumptions which underlie the periodic financial accounts of business enterprises. At the present time the four following fundamental concepts (the relative importance of which will vary according to the circumstances of the particular case) are regarded as having general acceptability:
>
> (a)    the "going concern" concept: the enterprise will continue in operational existence for the foreseeable future. This means in particular that the profit and loss account and balance sheet assume no intention or necessity to liquidate or curtail significantly the scale of operation;
>
> (b)    the "accruals" concept: revenue and costs are accrued (that is, recognised as they are earned or incurred, not as money is received or paid), matched with one another so far as their relationship can be established or justifiably assumed, and dealt with in the profit and loss account of the period to which they relate; provided that where the accruals concept is inconsistent with the "prudence" concept (paragraph (d) below), the latter prevails. The accruals concept implies that the profit and loss account reflects changes in the amount of net assets that arise out of the transactions of the relevant period (other than distributions or subscriptions of capital and unrealised surpluses arising on revaluation of fixed assets). Revenue and profits dealt with in the profit and loss account are matched with associated costs and expenses by including in the same account the costs incurred in earning them (so far as these are material and identifiable);
>
> (c)    the "consistency" concept: there is consistency of accounting treatment of like items within each accounting period and from one period to the next;
>
> (d)    the concept of "prudence"; revenue and profits are not anticipated, but are recognised by inclusion in the profit and loss account only when realised in the form either of cash or of other assets the ultimate cash realisation of which can be assessed with reasonable certainty; provision is made for all known liabilities (expenses and losses) whether the amount of these is known with certainty or is a best estimate in the light of the information available.'[6]

6. INSTITUTE OF CHARTERED ACCOUNTANTS IN ENGLAND AND WALES, Statement of Standard Accounting Practice, M2, para 14.

## 1.7 Revaluation of Assets

Although the transaction basis of recording assets is most common, examples may be found of other values being adopted. The downward revaluation of current assets has already been mentioned. In the case of stocks of commodities such as gold or tea there is a long-standing custom of using selling price less selling costs rather than cost;[7] work in progress of firms engaged in long term contracts in building and construction may include a valuation element. In recent years the practice of revaluation of land and buildings, and to a lesser extent plant and machinery and investments, has grown. In part this is due to the recognition that historic cost is not sufficiently informative and may mislead readers of the balance sheet in times when prices are rising. If a company holds property which has increased substantially in value it is obviously of interest to the shareholders to know about it and the clearest way of conveying the information is to show it in the balance sheet. In the case of investments in equity shares it gives recognition to the fact that an asset which naturally grows in value cannot be fairly represented by its original cost. Revaluation is an important topic with a number of aspects and a full discussion is deferred to Chapters 3 and 4.

## 1.8 Summary

The financial accounts are firmly based on the day to day records of transactions of the company. Such records are essential to the financial control of the firm and include detailed accounts of receipts and payments of money, sales of goods to customers, purchases from suppliers and so on. The Companies Act 1948 sections 147 and 331 make the keeping of appropriate records obligatory and lay down penalties for failure. Their prime purpose is not to form a basis for the annual balance sheet, profit and loss account and flow of funds statement, but to provide a means of financial control in day to day operations. Nevertheless, the annual accounts are, in the main, summaries of such detailed records. By the use of precedent and standard rules the accounts can be prepared rapidly and economically

---

7. INSTITUTE OF CHARTERED ACCOUNTANTS IN ENGLAND AND WALES, Recommendations on Accounting Principles, N22, para 20.

with a minimum of personal judgement. In this sense the accounts are objective statements of the financial affairs of the company. There is however considerable room for personal judgement in the choice of precedent and valuation rules and to this extent one should regard the accounts as a subjective estimate of the financial results and position. The next chapter will explore some of the special problems which arise from this choice of treatment.

# 2 Variety in Accounting Methods

*'Income . . . Saving . . . Depreciation . . . rough approximations
used by the business man to steer himself through the bewildering changes
of situation which confront him.'*[1]

*2.1 Introduction—Reasons for Variety*

An examination of a number of sets of accounts will reveal considerable
variety in the way they are set out. In some balance sheets assets are
listed on the right-hand side of the page and liabilities on the left,
whilst in others the sides are reversed. Many companies adopt a
'vertical' form of presentation in which, for example, assets may be
listed first followed by capital and liabilities. Current liabilities may be
listed on the same side as long term liabilities or may be deducted
from current assets. Although custom and precedent tend to impose a
broadly similar pattern, and the main groups of assets and liabilities
are easily recognised, there is no standard form and companies are
free to design the statements as they think best. The Companies Acts
impose an obligation to report a great deal of information, but the
classifications adopted and the amount of detail disclosed can vary
depending on the judgement of the directors as to what is necessary
to give a true and fair view of the affairs of the company. What is not
so obvious from a brief glance at the accounts is that there are many

1. HICKS, J R, 'Value and Capital', Ch. XIV. Oxford University Press,
1946.

different methods of attaching money values to assets and liabilities. This is a major source of variety in accounts which affects not only the balance sheet but also the reported profit or loss, and the aim of this chapter will be to review some of the main differences in values which may be found. The 'Survey of Published Accounts' published annually by the Institute of Chartered Accountants in England and Wales is a valuable source of reference which will be used from time to time.

Three reasons for differences in valuation are considered in this and the next two chapters:

1.   The historic cost basis of accounts does not provide operative rules for dealing with each transaction in sufficient detail to produce a unique report. The same data can be treated in different ways according to the judgement of the person preparing the accounts, subject to a number of conventions and to precedents set in previous periods.

2.   Different transactions may be recorded in different ways because the legal form of the contract differs although in fact the practical result is the same or very similar.

3.   Although 'historic cost' is generally accepted as the basis of accounts it is not universally adopted. Companies are free to experiment with other ways of providing a picture of the financial situation, subject only to their providing the minimum information required by law. This has advantages and disadvantages. In the past many firms have used this freedom to develop more informative accounts; on the other hand comparison between companies is made more difficult by the variety of methods adopted. One major development has been the revaluation of fixed assets (particularly land and buildings) from time to time to provide a better indication of current values than is given by historic cost.

Variety in interpretation of historic cost can arise firstly in deciding what expenditure is attributable to an asset and secondly, in the case of fixed assets, in relating the cost of the asset to the periods during which the asset is used. The following examples are of general importance.

## 2.2 Stock in Trade and Work in Progress

The valuation of stock and work in progress provides a good example of the problem of deciding what expenditure is attributable to an asset. The conventional basis of stock valuation is cost or lower net realisable value (or possibly lower replacement value). Most items in stock will usually be valued at cost with a small number at the lower value. It has been suggested that the word 'valuation' should not be used.

> 'Many accountants dislike the use of the term "valuation" applied to the monetary amount at which inventories are stated in accounts, because they consider it imprecise and misleading. Throughout the English Institute's Recommendation "Treatment of stock-in-trade and work in progress in financial accounts", which is solely concerned with the subject, the term "valuation" is avoided; such terms as "the amount at which stock is stated" or "the amount at which stock is carried forward" are adopted instead.'[2]

Valuation is a convenient term, the alternatives are clumsy, and provided it is recognised that the 'valuation' is a conventional one there appears to be no harm in using it.

A full statement of the methods adopted in practice may be found in the English Institute's Recommendation[3] referred to in the above quotation, but two main problems can be identified. The most general problem is that of identifying the units in stock with the actual purchase of goods. In a few cases specific identification is possible but in many cases an average cost is calculated or goods are assumed to be related to purchases according to the order of their use—in Britain the first in first out (FIFO) basis identifies goods in stock with the later purchases in the period. Minor differences in value will arise according to the method used but one would not expect them to be significant. In the USA, on the other hand, some companies base the value on the assumption that the latest goods received have been used and that the cost of the stock is that of goods purchased earlier— possibly many years earlier—at relatively low prices. Although this

2. ACCOUNTANTS INTERNATIONAL STUDY GROUP, 'Accounting and Auditing Approaches to Inventories in Three Nations', 1968.
3. INSTITUTE OF CHARTERED ACCOUNTANTS IN ENGLAND AND WALES, 'Recommendation on Accounting Principles', N22.

last in first out (LIFO) method is not used in Britain it may affect the accounts of companies with American subsidiaries. The base stock method, which treats the initial stock as a fixed asset and the cost of replacing stock as it is used as an expense, is occasionally used and has effects similar to LIFO.

A more important problem arises in connection with the valuation of goods which have been manufactured or processed by the company, in which case it is necessary to identify the cost of processing as well as the cost of acquiring the materials and components. The elements of cost have been stated as follows:

'(a) direct expenditure on the purchase of goods bought for resale, and of materials and components used in the manufacture of finished goods.

(b) other direct expenditure which can be identified specifically as having been incurred in acquiring the stock or bringing it to its existing condition and location; examples are direct labour, transport, processing and packaging.

(c) such part, if any, of the overhead expenditure as is properly carried forward in the circumstances of the business instead of being charged against the revenue of the period in which it was incurred.'[4]

The overhead costs referred to in (c) may be treated in a variety of ways. They may be omitted altogether from the valuation. If included they will be limited in most cases to manufacturing costs— in particular selling, general administration and financial costs will normally be excluded. In some cases, such as long term contracts in building and civil engineering, the work in progress valuation may include all costs and, an exception to the historic cost rule, a proportion of the expected profit.

A large part of the overhead costs is fixed. They are incurred in providing manufacturing facilities of the required capacity and do not change automatically if production varies, at least within reasonable limits. This gives rise to two alternative interpretations of 'cost per unit' to be used for stock valuation.

4. INSTITUTE OF CHARTERED ACCOUNTANTS IN ENGLAND AND WALES, 'Recommendation on Accounting Principles', N22, paragraph 4.

1.   Total manufacturing costs should be spread over all units produced, according to some measure of the use of facilities, so that units in stock have the same cost as units sold. In other words goods are valued at an average cost and all identical units have the same cost.

2.   Production is regarded as consisting of two parts; that part which was sold in the period and that part which was put into stock. The first part had to be produced to maintain the level of sales but the production of the second part could have been deferred to the next period. Because the decision to produce for stock does not increase the fixed overhead costs it may be argued that no part of such costs should be allocated to the stock. The real cost is confined to the additional costs incurred because of the decision and hence to variable costs only.

We therefore have two main bases of arriving at the cost of stock and work in progress.

1.   Full cost in which a proportion of overhead costs is included.

2.   Marginal or direct cost which excludes fixed overhead costs.

The method of valuation based on cost may give rise to a variety of results. Standard, or budgeted, costs may be used as an approximation to actual costs. The apportionment of overhead cost may be based on the normal volume of operations, rather than the actual volume achieved during the period, to prevent the combination of fixed cost and changing volume from creating a variable cost per unit. Overhead costs may be identified with units of product by more or less elaborate methods, ranging from a single average rate applied to the direct labour cost of each unit, to a system of apportioning costs to cost centres first and calculating a separate rate for each centre to be applied to units processed in that centre. At each stage there are judgements to be made which affect the cost of goods in stock. However, the variations which occur because of the nature of the valuation method are unlikely to be large compared with the difference between full cost and marginal cost valuations.

*2.3 The Effects of Stock Valuation*

The reason for concern with the effects of stock valuation is that whilst the choice of method is fairly arbitrary, the results may be material to the understanding of the financial position. The importance of stocks in company balance sheets may be seen in the summaries given in Table 2.1. If a substantial portion of costs are fixed overhead costs, then the basis of stock valuation makes a significant difference to the asset structure. For example, if one-third of the stocks of engineering companies consist of overhead costs, then a change to marginal cost valuation would reduce the assets in Table 2.1 by £63 million, which is nearly 15% of the total assets less current liabilities.

*Table 2.1 Company Assets*

| | All groups (£m) | (%) | Engineering (66 companies) (£m) | (%) |
|---|---|---|---|---|
| Land and property | 2041 | 29 | 108 | 16 |
| Plant and equipment | 1032 | 15 | 125 | 19 |
| Trade investments | 184 | 3 | 8 | 1 |
| Intangible assets | 318 | 5 | 23 | 4 |
| Stocks | 1547 | 22 | 188 | 29 |
| Debtors | 1470 | 21 | 182 | 28 |
| Liquid assets | 383 | 5 | 22 | 3 |
| | 6975 | 100 | 656 | 100 |
| Current liabilities | 2097 | 30 | 225 | 34 |
| | 4878 | 70 | 431 | 66 |

*Source: Economist.* Industrial Profits and Assets. July/September 1969. Column 1 is a summation of the balance sheets of 446 companies in 23 industries (including property companies) producing results in the 3rd quarter of 1969.

Because the balance sheet and the profit and loss account are directly coupled, the change in the fixed cost component of stock directly affects the profit, but the effect is only likely to be material if the quantity of stock at the end of a period is substantially different from that at the beginning. If a marginal cost basis of valuation is adopted, a change in stock has no effect on profit because the change merely reflects the expenditure incurred or saved. If a full cost basis is used an increase in stock represents more than the additional cost incurred in producing it, because of the fixed cost component, and vice versa. This means that an increase in stock increases profit and a reduction in stock reduces profit compared with the result achieved with a stable stock. Thus the full cost basis of stock valuation shows higher profits than the marginal cost basis when stock increases and lower profits when it decreases. This is illustrated in Example 1 which is simplified by assuming there are no expenses other than those of manufacturing.

*Example 1*

COMPARISON BETWEEN FULL COST AND MARGINAL COST STOCK VALUATION

|  | *Full Cost* | | *Marginal Cost* | |
|---|---|---|---|---|
|  | (£) | (£) | (£) | (£) |
| Sales: 900 units at £10 each |  | 9,000 |  | 9,000 |
| Cost of making 1200 units |  |  |  |  |
| Variable costs | 4,800 |  | 4,800 |  |
| Fixed costs | 2,400 |  | 2,400 |  |
|  | 7,200 |  | 7,200 |  |
| Less cost of 300 units in stock | 1,800 | 5,400 | 1,200 | 6,000 |
| Profit |  | 3,600 |  | 3,000 |

In this example if production had been limited to 900 units the cost would have been £6,000 and the profit £3,000. Thus the marginal cost result is similar to that which would be shown by either method if production and sales were equal.

The lack of criteria to guide in the choice of method was illustrated by an enquiry made by the Scottish Institute of Chartered Accountants.[5] Out of 302 companies which responded, 21% included

5. RESEARCH AND PUBLICATIONS COMMITTEE OF SCOTTISH INSTITUTE OF CHARTERED ACCOUNTANTS, 'Valuation of Stock and Work in Progress' (1968).

no overhead cost in stock, 43% included factory cost only, and 36% included administration as well as factory cost. For work in progress the proportions were 28, 38 and 34% respectively. There was no evidence that the method used was related to the type of industry or the size of the company.

*2.4 Fixed Assets*

The statement of fixed assets, such as plant and machinery, at cost requires the identification of expenditure with the asset. In the case of purchase from, and installation by, an outside supplier and contractor this is a straightforward analysis of the purchase records. All costs of purchase, delivery and installation will be regarded as the cost of the asset and will be recorded as an addition to the appropriate class of fixed asset according to the classification scheme adopted. In other cases the cost may not be so well defined. In particular, problems may arise:

1.    When plant is constructed by the company rather than by an outside contractor.

2.    When new plant requires extensive running in during which it is unprofitable even though it may be producing.

3.    When grants and subsidies are received for the acquisition of plant.

In the first case the problem is similar to that discussed in the context of stock valuation. Should the company adopt a full cost or a marginal cost basis of valuation; in other words, to what extent, if any, should fixed overhead costs be apportioned to the cost of the assets constructed?

In the second case the question to be decided is, at what point of time do operations cease to be running in of plant and become normal production? Usually this will be a gradual process and the choice of a particular point of time will be fairly arbitrary. One solution, which may be adopted, is to treat construction costs as the cost of plant and subsequent costs, up to the time when it is judged that normal production has commenced, as development costs. The development costs may be written off as expenses as they are incurred or carried forward for a limited period, substantially less than the life of the plant.

In the case of subsidies for the purchase of assets the choice is between deducting the grant from the purchase price, to show the net amount as the cost of the asset, and treating the grant as a profit to be added to reserves, whilst showing the asset in the balance sheet at its gross cost. If the grant is treated as a profit then the alternative of bringing it into profit and loss account in instalments over the life of the asset or taking it straight into reserves as a special profit without its affecting annual trading profits are both possible. The result of a review of the treatment of investment grants by 300 companies is shown in Table 2.2

*Table 2.2 Treatment of Investment Grants*[6]

|                                                                                                                         | Number of Companies |
| ----------------------------------------------------------------------------------------------------------------------- | ------------------- |
| Grants deducted from the purchase price of assets                                                                       | 157                 |
| Grants being brought into the profit and loss account by instalments (in the meantime shown as deferred credits or reserves in the balance sheet) | 78                  |
| Other methods                                                                                                           | 16                  |
| No reference made to investment grants                                                                                  | 49                  |
|                                                                                                                         | ——                  |
|                                                                                                                         | 300                 |

Although investment grants were discontinued on 26 October 1970, the effects of the different treatments will remain in company balance sheets for many years and capital grants under the Industry Act 1972 give rise to similar problems.

*2.5 Depreciation of Fixed Assets*

With the exception of freehold land, fixed assets have a limited life and their cost (less any amount realised when they are finally disposed of) must be apportioned to the years which benefit from their use.

6. INSTITUTE OF CHARTERED ACCOUNTANTS IN ENGLAND AND WALES, 'Survey of Published Accounts 1969–70', p. 73. The main methods of treatment of grants are listed on page 72 and reveal minor variations on the main alternatives.

The asset is written down year by year in the balance sheet and the profit and loss account is charged with the annual depreciation expense. In a few cases other methods may be adopted; for example loose tools may be put into the balance sheet at original cost and the cost of renewals treated as expense when incurred. The depreciation charge in any year is obviously an estimate. It depends on the view taken by the directors of the expected life of assets and of the realisable value at the end of that life, although this may not be a material factor. It depends also on the interpretation of the basic concept of matching costs and revenues. This concept is poorly defined even in theory and has been interpreted in two ways:

1.     In terms of relating depreciation to the pattern of net revenues expected by the company. What is meant by net revenue is not clearly defined.

2.     In terms of calculating depreciation in such a way as to provide a constant ratio of profit to capital employed. For example:

'One of the most relevant arguments for the sinking fund method is that it permits a public utility to earn a constant rate of return on its total investment when its revenue is held constant through regulation.'[7]

The sinking fund method is essentially the same as the annuity method of depreciation referred to below.

In practice the choice is made between several traditional patterns which may be summarised as follows:

1.     Straight line, in which equal annual instalments are written off. For an asset costing £10,000 with an estimated life of 10 years and no residual value the annual charge is £1,000.

2.     Declining charge, in which the depreciation written off in each year is less than that in the preceding year. The most common declining charge method, the reducing balance method, calculates depreciation as a fixed percentage of the book value of the asset, that is, the cost less depreciation written off in previous years.

7. HENDRIKSEN, E S, 'Accounting Theory', Irwin (1970), p. 409.

A depreciation rate of $2/n$ where $n$ is the number of years in
the expected total life of the asset is regarded as appropriate,[8]
which means that the first year's depreciation is double the
charge using the straight line method. In the above example
the rate of depreciation is 20 per cent, giving a charge of £2,000
in year 1, £1,600 in year 2, and so on.

3. Increasing charge, or annuity method, which produces a smaller
charge in the early years compared with later years, the rate of
increase being equal to the rate of interest assumed in the
calculation. Using a rate of 10 per cent, annuity depreciation is
£628 in year 1, £690 in year 2 and increasing by 10 per cent
in each successive year.

4. Depletion methods which seek to relate the charge to a
measure of use of the asset; to materials extracted from a quarry
(as a proportion of the total contents) or flying hours of an
aircraft (as a proportion of total expected flying hours over
the life of the plane).

*Table 2.3 Methods of Depreciation*[9]

|                                  | Number of Companies | |
|                                  | 1970–71 | 1969–70 |
|----------------------------------|---------|---------|
| Basis adopted for most assets:   |         |         |
| Straight line                    | 96      | 81      |
| Reducing balance                 | 1       | 4       |
| Mixture of methods               | 17      | 13      |
|                                  | 114     | 98      |
| Basis not disclosed              | 186     | 202     |
|                                  | 300     | 300     |

8. Theoretically the rate is $1 - \sqrt[n]{R/C}$ where $C$ is the cost of the asset,
$R$ is the value of the asset at the end of its economic life, and $n$ is the
number of years in that life; but this calculation does not seem to be
used in practice, and if there is no residual value $(R)$ the resulting rate
of 100% would be regarded as unreasonable.

9. INSTITUTE OF CHARTERED ACCOUNTANTS IN ENGLAND AND WALES,
'Survey of Published Accounts 1970–71', p. 32.

The straight line method appears to be the most commonly adopted as can be seen from Table 3.

The choice of depreciation method has a significant influence on the accounts. If a company remained the same size and renewed an equal amount of assets in each year and prices were stable, the depreciation charge would be the same in each year whether the company used straight line, reducing balance or annuity method. In the normal situation of growth and rising prices the declining charge methods tend to produce a higher depreciation charge and lower profits than the straight line method, which in turn charges more than the annuity method. Even if profits are not affected, the total assets in

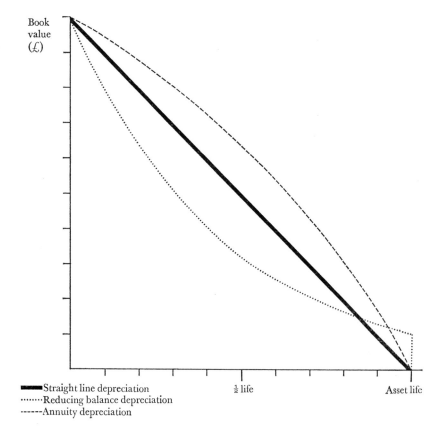

■■■■Straight line depreciation                          ½ life                          Asset life
········Reducing balance depreciation
------Annuity depreciation

*Figure 2.1   Book Value of Assets*

the balance sheet will be materially affected. When one-half of the life of an asset is expired the book value using the straight line method is one-half of its cost (assuming the saleable value at the end of its life is negligible). Using reducing balance method the book value is approximately one-third of cost at the half life. The decline in book value is illustrated in Figure 2.1. As the choice of depreciation policy is fairly arbitrary knowledge of the methods used may be important in appraising the results of the company.

## 2.6 Intangible Assets

A class of assets which causes exceptional difficulty is that consisting of assets such as goodwill and the results of research and development; attitudes, qualities and knowledge rather than tangible machines, buildings and vehicles. The category of intangibles is not precisely defined and should be regarded as a useful appellation for certain fixed assets, for which the normal methods of valuation by reference to cost and a regular pattern of depreciation are not very appropriate. An important characteristic, in addition to the lack of corporeal existence, is that of a high degree of uncertainty as to the cost of acquiring the asset or of the benefits attaching to it at any point of time, and therefore as to the amount which should appear in the balance sheet. A lease of land is intangible in that it is a right to undisturbed use rather than ownership of the land itself. Nevertheless, it carries with it possession of a very tangible asset for a precise period of time, and if it is acquired by payment of a lump sum, that sum is the cost of the asset which may be depreciated (or amortised) over the period of the lease. Whilst some accountants regard a lease as an intangible asset others would not distinguish it from other fixed assets. The nature and uncertainties of intangibles may be identified by examples.

Goodwill may be defined briefly as the power to earn profits in excess of a normal return on the tangible assets and may therefore be said to comprise all intangible assets. If goodwill is purchased its cost is normally identified as the difference between the total price paid for a business and the sum of the amounts identified as the cost of other assets such as plant, stocks, et cetera. Although the cost is known the life of the asset is uncertain, and the basis of a regular policy of amortisation is missing. In practice the treatment of such goodwill varies from the immediate writing off of the full amount by deduction from reserves to the carrying forward of the full amount as an asset indefinitely. No special significance can be attached to either treatment. The elimination of the asset from the balance sheet does not indicate that it is of no value any more than the inclusion of the asset indicates the continuation of the goodwill. The fact that goodwill is not purchased does not mean that it does not exist; it will often be created internally by good management or by good luck. Some specific costs such as staff training and marketing may be identifiable, but others are inseparable from the day to day costs of running the business. In practice, therefore the cost of goodwill created within the business is not brought into the balance sheet.

*Research and Development* expenditure creates two problems— what is the cost and what is the benefit? At first sight the cost of research should not be difficult to ascertain but the superficial view omits one important point. Research is often undertaken with the expectation that only a proportion of the experiments will be successful and produce worthwhile commercial development. This is so whether one is dealing with the search for oil or research into new drugs. In these circumstances is it reasonable to write off the cost of expenditure identified with unsuccessful projects as an expense and capitalise, or treat as the cost of the asset, only that which is identified with successful projects? Alternatively on what basis are costs of the research programme to be apportioned to successful projects? The difficulty is increased when knowledge of the commercial success, or otherwise, of discoveries is delayed for several years after the discovery is made, as it is in the case of new drugs. Because the question of how much expenditure to show in the balance sheet as the cost of the asset turns on an assessment of potential benefits, which are highly uncertain and may not be realised for many years, the normal practice is to write off research expenditure as an expense in the year in which it is incurred. In some cases, usually those relating to development expenditure the fruits of which can be anticipated within a short period of time, the cost may be capitalised and amortised over a short period of three or four years. It would be unusual to carry forward the asset for an extended period.

The Survey of Published Accounts 1970–71[10] identifies 53 instances in which research and development expenditure is mentioned in the accounts of 42 companies out of the 300 companies included in the survey. In only ten instances was expenditure capitalised and eight of these refer to fixed and current assets used in research. In other words in the 42 companies which can be identified as carrying on research only two brought the intangible assets into the balance sheet, the other eight instances being records of tangible plant and stores used in research. This may not fully indicate the extent to which research is treated as an expense, because there is no need for companies to disclose the amount spent and written off.

The existence of intangible assets, for which reliable valuation procedures do not exist, creates a gap in the information provided by the accounts. A company may have assets of considerable value which are not represented at all in the balance sheet. It may also to some extent manage the amount of its profit by varying this investment type expenditure and so reducing or increasing its expenses from period to period. It is interesting to quote Sir Alan Wilson, the Chairman of Glaxo Group Ltd in this context. After discussing at length the company's research programme he said,

'It would, of course, be possible to increase the profits of the Company considerably in the short run by diminishing our research, but we are sure that the long term effects would be fatal, and we are, indeed, planning to increase our research very substantially over the next five to seven years.'[11]

The Company writes off the whole of the research expenditure as it is incurred.

## 2.7 Taxation

The treatment of taxation of profits is an important example of the possibility of different interpretations of the concept of matching cost

10. INSTITUTE OF CHARTERED ACCOUNTANTS IN ENGLAND AND WALES, 'Survey of Published Accounts 1970–71', p. 42.
11. GLAXO GROUP LTD, 'Annual Report for the Year Ended 30 June 1969', p. 6.

C.P.C.A.—D

with revenue. Corporation tax is charged on company profits calculated according to normal commercial principles but with statutory modifications. One difference between profits shown in the profit and loss account and profit on which tax is based is due to the provision of incentives to invest in fixed assets and research by allowing more rapid writing off (or depreciation) than is normally accepted in the accounts. Thus from 21 March 1972 expenditure on the purchase of machinery and plant may be treated entirely as an expense at the time it is incurred, irrespective of the life of the plant, for the purpose of calculating tax on profits. The result of this is best illustrated by an example of the effect of purchasing a machine. A very short life of two years is assumed to simplify the illustration.

*Example 2.* A machine costing £1,000 is to be depreciated over two years on the straight line method. Profits before depreciation are £1,200 per annum. The corporation tax calculation would be as follows (assuming no other modifications to accounting profit are necessary).

|  | Year 1 (£) | Year 2 (£) |
|---|---|---|
| Profit before depreciation | 1,200 | 1,200 |
| Allowance for new machine | 1,000 | — |
|  | 200 | 1,200 |
| Corporation Tax at 40% | £ 80 | £480 |

If the accounts of the company were to show the strict liability for tax, the profit and loss account would be as follows:

|  | Year 1 (£) | Year 2 (£) |
|---|---|---|
| Profit before depreciation | 1,200 | 1,200 |
| Depreciation | 500 | 500 |
| Net profit before tax | 700 | 700 |

Corporation Tax on the profits of
the year                                           80            480

                                                   ‾‾‾‾          ‾‾‾‾
                                                   620           220
                                                   ====          ====

Because the tax is not due for payment until after the end of the financial year the sum of £80 would appear as a liability in the balance sheet at the end of year 1 and the sum of £480 at the end of year 2.

An alternative interpretation is that the tax is only deferred by the acceleration of the writing off of the asset. The low tax charge in year 1 is compensated by the high tax charge in year 2 when no depreciation allowance is obtained. The accounts should recognize this by charging in the profit and loss account the amount of tax which would have been payable if a normal depreciation charge had been made. In other words an attempt should be made to match the taxation charge with the profit as shown by the profit and loss account. If this interpretation were followed the taxation charge to the profit and loss account would be modified as follows:

|                                 |        | Year 1 (£) |        | Year 2 (£) |
| ------------------------------- | ------ | ---------- | ------ | ---------- |
| Net profit before tax           |        | 700        |        | 700        |
| Corporation Tax on the profits  |        |            |        |            |
| of the year                     | 80     |            | 480    |            |
| Adjust deferred tax             | +200   | 280        | −200   | 280        |
|                                 | ‾‾‾‾   | ‾‾‾‾       | ‾‾‾‾   | ‾‾‾‾       |
| Net profit after tax            |        | 420        |        | 420        |
|                                 |        | ====       |        | ====       |

The balance sheet at the end of year 1 would then be modified to show the deferred liability of £200 (sometimes called the taxation equalisation account) in addition to the current liability of £80. It will be noted that this is not a liability which is certain in amount and payable on a given date. At the end of year 1 it is contingent upon the company continuing to make profits and on the taxation law, including the rate of tax, in the future.[12] It is not a liability which *must* be brought into account, although the Institute of Chartered Accountants has recommended that it should.

> 'A deferred taxation account should be established and maintained at current rates of taxation whenever there exist material taxation liabilities which may crystallise at some future date on profits and surpluses already bought into account.'[13]

A large number of companies adopt the recommendation of the Institute—the Survey of Published Accounts 1970–71[14] shows 204 companies out of 300 with deferred taxation accounts—but because companies may choose either to ignore deferred taxation or to bring it into account it is necessary to ascertain which method has been used when reading the accounts. Care may be needed in interpreting the terms used in that 'deferred taxation' in a balance sheet may in some cases refer to the legal tax liability on the current years profits, if it falls due for payment more than 12 months after the balance sheet. For example in the case of a company with a financial year ending between 6 April 1971 and 31 December 1971, taxation for the year is normally payable on 1 January 1973. In the 1971 balance sheet this may be grouped with current liabilities or may be recorded separately, in which case it may be termed a deferred liability, although the sum is fixed and known. In the figures quoted from the Survey of Published Accounts such liability is not treated as deferred tax.

Deferred taxation may also arise when assets are restated at a valuation higher than cost. Such revaluation creates an unrealised

12. The change in the basis of taxation of companies in 1973 will mean a substantial increase in the rate of tax on profit, so that an increase in deferred tax may be made in accounts dated after the change. The complexity of the problem can be appreciated when it is understood that this does not necessarily represent an additional burden to the shareholder because the increase in the company's tax rate will be offset by the change in taxation of dividends.

13. INSTITUTE OF CHARTERED ACCOUNTANTS IN ENGLAND AND WALES, 'Recommendation on Accounting Principles', N27. para 33(a).

14. INSTITUTE OF CHARTERED ACCOUNTANTS IN ENGLAND AND WALES, 'Survey of Published Accounts 1970–71', p. 113.

profit or surplus which is not taxable until realised. A company may nevertheless indicate that such a surplus does not wholly represent a gain to shareholders by deducting tax, which is shown as deferred taxation—that is, instead of recording a single sum being the surplus on revaluation, this sum is split into two parts:

1.    The tax which would be paid if the asset were sold at that price.

2.    The balance representing the net of tax gain to the shareholders. As in the case of the adjustment for accelerated depreciation allowances on fixed assets such as plant, this deferred tax is dependent on future events and is not a fixed, determined amount. It may, therefore, be adjusted from time to time as tax rates change.

*2.8 The Legal Form of Transactions*
The effect of legal form on the recording of a transaction must be mentioned because it may have important implications for the interpretation of accounts. One example, of a specialised nature, is the difference in recording revenue between different types of selling agreements. A company which sells goods for which the customer pays by instalments usually brings the full cash price into the profit and loss account at the time of sale. A company which disposes of goods on hire purchase terms, in which the ownership of the goods does not pass until the end of the term of the agreement, usually brings into the profit and loss account as revenue only the rentals or instalments payable in the period. In the balance sheet the asset related to the first transaction is a debtor, representing the balance of the selling price unpaid; the asset related to the second transaction is a stock of goods out on hire purchase at a valuation based on cost. The hire purchase form of the transaction delays the taking into account of profit and reduces the amount of assets shown in the balance sheet as compared with the credit sale. However, the results of the transactions are practically identical from the company's point of view—goods have been disposed of to customers who pay for them over an extended period of time.

An example of more general application is the acquisition of assets by a company. If a company buys a machine outright it is recorded as a fixed asset at cost, less depreciation. If money is borrowed to pay for the machine the outstanding loan is classified as a liability. If the machine is acquired under a hire purchase agreement it is recorded in a similar way, except that the unpaid portion of the cost is likely to be deducted from the book value in the balance sheet, although it may be grouped with liabilities. An alternative method of acquiring fixed assets is to lease them on terms which give the company full use of the asset for its economic life. It undertakes to pay the finance company the full cost of the machine plus financing charges, which in total are similar to the cost of hire purchase after taking tax allowances into account. Although the company never owns the machine it may receive credit for any sale proceeds which are realised so that the practical results are the same. In the balance sheet however no record is made of either the asset or the liability to pay future rentals. The rental payable is treated as an expense in the period for which it is paid. The main effect of leasing assets is to show a smaller total of assets in the balance sheet and smaller liabilities than in the case of purchase. It also modifies the pattern of profits because, although the lease rentals are equivalent in total to depreciation plus interest, the timing of the charge to profit and loss account is not the same. As the ratio of profit/total assets is frequently used in comparing the results of companies the effect may be significant and it has been mooted that leases should be treated in a similar way to bought assets in order to improve comparability.

### 2.9 Summary

In this chapter an attempt has been made to illustrate some of the more important ways in which variety of method of recording transactions can arise and the reasons for this. Whilst the main aspects have been mentioned the treatment is not exhaustive and reference should be made to the annual Survey of Published Accounts for a more detailed statement of what is happening in practice. One aspect has not been illustrated at all—the abandonment of strict historic cost records and the introduction of valuation of assets. This will be dealt with in the discussion of the effects of price changes in Chapter 3 and of investments in Chapter 4.

# 3 Price Changes

*'We note that a seemingly simple statement of the condition of a firm at a given date is in fact a very complicated matter and subject to the occurrence of many errors whose nature and amount are usually shrouded in mystery.'*[1]

## 3.1 Introduction—Interpretation

Accounting reports are historical statements; they are generally based on costs derived from recorded transactions because such records provide objective evidence of value at a specific time. The reports are not, however, simply lists of transactions. They are intended to provide an interpretation of history and are used to assess the position and profitability of the firm. The reader is concerned with the meaning of the figures and what lies behind them, not with the figures just as numbers. If prices were stable the meaning of the statements would be much clearer because 'cost' would be timeless. Total cost of fixed assets would represent the current cost of buying an equivalent set of fixed assets and would therefore be a good indicator of the value of those assets. Similarly depreciation charged in the profit and loss account would approximate to the amount which would have to be spent to maintain the same quantity of assets—if the company remained the same size and replaced an equal proportion of its fixed assets in each year the depreciation charge would equal the amount spent on replacement.

1. MORGENSTERN, O, 'On the Accuracy of Economic Observations,' Ch. 4.

43

When prices change materially the numbers used in the accounts only represent the underlying transactions when the dates of the transactions are attached. 'Land at cost £10,000' has a different meaning depending on whether the purchase was in 1900 or in 1970. If transactions on different dates are added together it may be impossible to give a reasonable interpretation of the result. It is meaningful to state that a company owns a plot of land which cost £10,000 in 1900 and a building erected on the land at a cost of £1 million in 1970 but much less useful to state that freehold property owned by the company cost £1,010,000. This criticism applies to the treatment of fixed assets in the balance sheet and to the depreciation charged in the profit and loss account which contains a similar mixture of historic costs. It also applies to the numbers labelled 'total assets', 'profit' and any items which purport to represent a series of transactions at widely separated dates.

One way of using accounts is to compare events of different periods and identify changes taking place over time. Consider the interpretation of the following trend of sales:

|            | *Revenue* |
|------------|-----------|
| Period 1   | £104,000  |
| Period 2   | £107,120  |
| Period 3   | £112,320  |
| Period 4   | £115,440  |

If prices are stable this increasing trend represents increasing quantities sold and is a measure of expansion of activity. If prices are rising, however, the interpretation is obscure and needs to be made clearer by identifying the separate effects of price and volume. If there is only one product this may be done by showing both quantities and revenue; if there are several products it will be necessary to devise other methods using price indices. In the above example the knowledge of average price per unit, would enable the reader to identify the quantities sold, the statement of both revenue and prices in index form would make the comparison clearer, the adjustment of revenue by the price index would show sales at constant prices and so reveal the underlying trend of volume without further calculation by the reader.

*Example 1*

| Period | (1)<br>Sales<br>revenue<br>(£) | (2)<br>Price per<br>unit<br>(£) | (3)<br>Index of<br>sales<br>revenue | (4)<br><br>Price<br>index | (5)<br>Sales adjusted<br>by price index<br>= col. 1 × 100<br>col. 4 |
|---|---|---|---|---|---|
| 1 | 104,000 | 4.00 | 100 | 100 | 104,000 |
| 2 | 107,120 | 4.12 | 103 | 103 | 104,000 |
| 3 | 112,320 | 4.32 | 108 | 108 | 104,000 |
| 4 | 115,440 | 4.44 | 111 | 111 | 104,000 |

Thus in Example 1 comparison of columns 1 and 2 indicates that the rise in revenue is partly due to rising prices but without calculation the relative contributions of price and volume are not obvious. By comparing columns 3 and 4, in which revenue and price in period 1 are both stated at the same base of 100 and subsequent increases related to this base, it is clearly seen that the increase in sales is due entirely to increase in price. Column 5, which expresses sales in constant prices of period 1, shows that no change in quantity has occurred and is a useful way of presenting the same information. If one is dealing with a financial statement such as a flow of funds statement, in which the transactions all refer to a comparatively short period of time, the reader can make a rough allowance for price changes in examining trends over several periods, although his task is simplified by the provision of adjusted figures. In the case of the balance sheet, which reflects a mixture of transactions which have occurred at different times, the problem is much more difficult.

*3.2 Finance and Inflation*

In Example 2 the accounts of a company are drawn up on the normal historic cost basis at two different dates. The company is stable in size; its fixed assets have a life of 15 years and one-fifteenth are replaced in each year so that the number and composition of assets is constant. The quantities of stock held are constant, the same terms of credit are given to customers and received from suppliers and the physical volume of sales and purchases is unchanged from year to year. All prices have increased at a constant rate of 5% per annum for the last 15 years. The differences between the two balance sheets are solely due to changes in prices. Although the assets employed are the same the balance sheets tend to suggest growth in size of 5% during year 2.

*Example 2*

COMPARATIVE BALANCE SHEETS drawn up on the historic cost basis during a period of rising prices. (Price increase 5% per annum.

Life of fixed assets 15 years.)

|  | *Year* | | | *Year* | |
|---|---|---|---|---|---|
|  | *1* (£) | *2* (£) |  | *1* (£) | *2* (£) |
| Capital & reserves | 22,300 | 24,200 | Fixed assets | 18,300 | 19,200 |
| Loan | 15,000 | 15,000 | Current assets: | | |
|  |  |  | Stock | 15,200 | 16,000 |
|  |  |  | Debtors & cash | 22,800 | 24,000 |
|  |  |  |  | 38,000 | 40,000 |
|  |  |  | Less creditors | 19,000 | 20,000 |
|  |  |  |  | 19,000 | 20,000 |
|  | £37,300 | 39,200 | Total assets | £37,300 | 39,200 |

It is instructive to examine this illustration in the context of the financing of the company. Profit is normally regarded as a surplus which can be distributed without disturbing the financial position so that if profit is retained it is available to finance expansion. In the illustration, capital and reserves have increased by £1,900, i.e. profits of this amount have been retained, although the underlying asset situation is unchanged. In other words the profit shown as earned during the year is not available for distribution in full if the financial position is to be maintained. The additional finance required is made up as follows:

| | (£) |
|---|---|
| Excess of the cost of replacement of fixed assets over the amount charged for depreciation | 900 |
| Additional finance needed to maintain stock | 800 |
| Additional finance for debtors | 1,200 |
| | 2,900 |
| Less additional finance supplied by creditors | 1,000 |
| | 1,900 |

On average if prices continue to rise at the rate of 5% per annum the company must each year continue to retain profits, or find alternative finance equal to 5% of its total assets in order to maintain the same size.

Example 3 shows the same balance sheets adjusted by a price index so that all assets and liabilities are expressed in terms of prices in year 2. Because all prices have risen by 5% per annum the value of the monetary unit may be regarded as having fallen in the sense that £1 in year 2 will buy less than £1 in year 1. The adjustment of the loan in year 1 recognises the fact that at that time its purchasing power was equivalent to £15,800 spent in year 2. The adjusted balance sheet shows clearly that the company has not changed in size and that the only real change is that the loan holders supply a relatively smaller proportion of the total capital (they have lost £800 because of inflation) and the shareholders have increased their proportion to compensate.

*Example 3*

BALANCE SHEETS from Example 2 adjusted to prices ruling at year 2.

|  | Year 1 (£) | Year 2 (£) |  | Year 1 (£) | Year 2 (£) |
|---|---|---|---|---|---|
| Capital & reserves | 28,000 | 28,800 | Fixed assets | 23,800 | 23,800 |
| Loan | 15,800 | 15,000 | Current assets: | | |
|  |  |  | Stock | 16,000 | 16,000 |
|  |  |  | Debtors & cash | 24,000 | 24,000 |
|  |  |  |  | 40,000 | 40,000 |
|  |  |  | Less creditors | 20,000 | 20,000 |
|  |  |  |  | 20,000 | 20,000 |
|  | £43,800 | 43,800 | Total assets | £43,800 | 43,800 |

This is of course a relatively simple example. In practice prices of different goods and services change in different ways, the nature and quality of goods and services change so that measurement of price changes is complicated. Nevertheless, unless price changes are very small it is obvious that failure to make allowance for them seriously affects the understanding of a company's financial position.

*3.3 Ratios and Inflation*

One way of obtaining an insight into the financial structure and the results of a company is to examine a number of ratios. A favourite ratio is return on capital which may be calculated by relating net profit plus interest on loans to total assets. If net profits and total assets are taken directly from the historic cost accounts the ratio is at best an extremely crude indicator because of the defects in both of its components. If one were to compare return on capital after a period of rising prices, with the same ratio calculated from accounts expressed in terms of current prices one would find that the historic accounts would show a higher profit and lower total assets. The ratio is highly distorted because both errors affect it in the same way. In Example 2 if profit according to the historic accounts is taken as £7,500, return on capital is £7,500/39,200 = 19.1%. To calculate the ratio on the basis of current prices one must adjust the profit by £1,900 which is the amount of additional finance which the company requires to maintain the same size. An adjusted profit and loss account would show additional depreciation, based on current costs, of £900, additional cost of sales £800 and net loss from financing debtors, of £200. From the ordinary shareholders point of view there is also a gain of £800 from loan finance, but from the point of view of the company as a whole this is directly offset by the loss to the lenders. The return on capital in current terms is therefore £5,600/43,800 = 12.8%, which is significantly different from the unadjusted return of 19.1%. Distortion of ratios will occur whenever the amounts used are based on transactions occurring at different dates. Even small rates of change in prices may have a material effect. In this illustration 5% inflation was sufficient to create an adjustment of depreciation by £900—an increase of about 45% if depreciation was calculated on the straight line basis—and a profit adjustment of 25%.

*3.4 Revaluation of Assets*

The problems of using accounts based on historic cost have been recognised for a long time but a solution which is generally acceptable has not been found. In 1952 the Institute of Chartered Accountants in England and Wales issued a statement on the subject containing the following conclusion.

'The Council cannot emphasise too strongly that the significance of accounts prepared on the basis of historical cost is subject to limitations, not the least of which is that the monetary unit in which the accounts are prepared is not a stable unit of measurement. In consequence the results shown by accounts prepared on the basis of historical cost are not a measure of increase or decrease in wealth in terms of purchasing power; nor do the results necessarily represent the amount which can prudently be regarded as available for distribution, having regard to the financial requirements of the business. Similarly the results shown by such accounts are not necessarily suitable for purposes such as price fixing, wage negotiations and taxation, unless in using them for these purposes due regard is paid to the amount of profit which has been retained in the business for its maintenance.

On the other hand the alternatives to historical cost which have so far been suggested appear to have serious defects and their logical application would raise social and economic issues going far beyond the realm of accountancy. The Council is therefore unable to regard any of the suggestions so far made as being acceptable alternatives to the existing accounting principles based on historical cost.'[2]

Despite the conclusion of the Institute, individual companies have attempted to improve their accounts by adjusting for the most obvious effect of price changes, the understatement of fixed assets. The long lives of such assets and especially of land and buildings, can cover periods of considerable price changes with the result that the total of assets in the balance sheet is not very meaningful. For many types of property there is a good market and valuation may be made with a fair degree of accuracy. Many companies have therefore adopted the practice of revaluing property from time to time and a smaller number of companies have revalued other fixed assets. For example a review of the accounts of 300 large companies[3] revealed that 205 had revalued property and 90 had revalued other fixed assets as shown on page 51.

It will be noted that all assets in any category may not be revalued in the same year but the sum of the assets may consist of some items at cost (at different dates) and others at valuations made at different dates. This could be extremely confusing, and the Companies Act 1967 (Sch. 2, para 11) helps to clarify the situation by requiring

2. INSTITUTE OF CHARTERED ACCOUNTANTS IN ENGLAND AND WALES, 'Recommendations on Accounting Principles', N15, para. 28 and 29.
3. INSTITUTE OF CHARTERED ACCOUNTANTS IN ENGLAND AND WALES, 'Survey of Published Accounts 1970–71', p. 76.

|                                                    | *Property* | *Other fixed assets (excluding investments)* |
|----------------------------------------------------|------------|----------------------------------------------|
| Revaluation, or the most recent in a series of revaluations, shown in: |            |                                              |
| Year of account or the previous four years         | 113        | 45                                           |
| Five or more years earlier                         | 86         | 43                                           |
| Year not specified                                 | 6          | 2                                            |
|                                                    | 205        | 90                                           |
| No material portion of fixed assets shown at a valuation | 95   | 210                                          |
|                                                    | 300        | 300                                          |

that the separate valuations and the year of each valuation be stated.

The effect of price changes on the profit and loss account has not been given much attention. Revaluation of plant and machinery increases the charge for depreciation and therefore reduces profit as compared with the result before revaluation. Revaluation of buildings on the other hand may increase depreciation (on the ground that the current year should bear its share of the expired value of an asset of limited life) or may be given as a reason for charging no depreciation at all (on the ground that if the asset continues to increase in value it is not depreciating). Although the basis adopted will be clear if the accounts are examined in detail, the possibility of alternative treatment of the same events increases the risk of confusion and misinterpretation, and reduces the possibility of making comparisons between different companies or even of comparing different periods in the same company's history. The effects of price changes other than those arising from depreciation of fixed assets are generally ignored. No attempt is made to charge the current cost of goods sold instead of the historic cost, although the American LIFO system of stock valuation does this in a rough and ready manner, nor to account for profits and losses from receiving and giving credit and holding cash assets. In general therefore profits tend to be inflated by the effects of price rises modified in individual cases by the increased charge for depreciation arising from the revaluation of all or part of the fixed assets.

### 3.5 Revaluation and Taxation

In Chapter 2 mention was made of the possible effect on deferred taxation of the revaluation of assets. The difference between the book value of an asset before revaluation and the new value is an increase in net assets, which must be reflected in an increase in reserves. If the asset is sold for the new value a liability for tax on the surplus may fall due for payment. The question is whether such potential liability can be ignored until it accrues or whether it should be indicated in the accounts, either as a provision for deferred taxation or simply by way of a note in the balance sheet. The Institute of Chartered Accountants has recommended[4] that either course may be adopted provided the potential liability continues to be stated in future accounts so long as it exists.

If a company revalues property standing in the books at £100,000, the following extracts from the balance sheet illustrate two alternatives, on the assumption that the full surplus would be taxable at 40% if realised. In column A no provision for deferred tax is made. In column B full provision is made and the surplus on revaluation is reduced accordingly. If the Institute's recommendation is followed a note would be included in the accounts A that there is a potential tax liability of £20,000.

BALANCE SHEET (extracts)

|  | A (£) | B (£) |
|---|---|---|
| Reserve: Surplus on revaluation of property | 50,000 | 30,000 |
| Deferred taxation |  | 20,000 |

The deferred taxation is not fixed in amount but will vary over time for two reasons.

4. INSTITUTE OF CHARTERED ACCOUNTANTS IN ENGLAND AND WALES, 'Recommendations on Accounting Principles', N27, para. 47.

1.   As taxation is payable at the rate in force when the gain is realised a change in the rate of tax will alter the estimate of potential liability.

2.   If the asset is being depreciated, the difference between depreciated historic cost and the new balance sheet value will diminish over time, so that the untaxed surplus included in the accounts diminishes. When the asset is finally put out of use and written off the potential tax liability is zero. The reserve entitled 'surplus on revaluation' will not normally be reduced because the additional depreciation caused by the revaluation will be deducted as an expense in the profit and loss account. If the company had not revalued, additional profits equal to the surplus on revaluation would have accumulated over the life of the asset, so that the total reserves would be the same at the end of that time, although they would exist wholly as undistributed profits rather than in part as surplus on revaluation. In other words it is only immediately after the revaluation of depreciating assets that the surplus on revaluation is entirely unrealised.

*3.6  Current Values in Accounts*
The present situation, in which some companies adjust some assets to current prices at intervals of time decided by the directors, is not very satisfactory. It increases the number of different ways in which the financial affairs of a company can be stated and reduces the comparability of accounts. It is widely recognised that a strict adherence to historic costs is not the right answer in times of continuously rising prices and two alternative methods have been suggested.

1.   The general use of current values in accounts.

2.   Retention of historic cost as a basis, but supplemented by statements in which the figures are converted into monetary units of constant value.

The use of current values is not intended to lead to the preparation of a balance sheet which values the company. The possibility of valuing intangible assets, such as goodwill, on a regular basis suitable for the annual accounts, is remote and in practice current valuation must be confined to those assets for which the current replacement cost, or realisable value, can be ascertained. The general rule of valuation may be stated as the lower of the cost of replacing the asset (or more precisely the services provided by the asset) or the net realisable value, where realisation may be outright sale or the realisation of benefits from the use of the asset. Replacement cost is supported as a proper basis of valuation on the grounds that, if the company did not have the use of the asset, it would either have to replace it or do without it. The decision would depend upon two quantities.

1.    The present value of the benefits expected to be realised from the use of the asset (including the possibility of sale).

2.    The cost of replacing the services provided by the asset.

If the benefits exceed the cost then the correct decision is to replace; if cost exceeds benefits then no replacement should be made. It follows that the maximum loss which a company suffers by not having an asset is the cost of replacing it, and the replacement cost is the maximum value which can be placed on that asset.

Although the use of current values is not without precedent—replacement costs have been used by N V Phillips[5] for many years and many Investment Trust Companies use market values—the method is not widely accepted by the accounting profession. From the auditors' point of view current value is not as objective a measure as historic cost, which can be verified by reference to the records of the transaction. Evidence of current value may vary in quality from the published prices of shares quoted on the Stock Exchange to historic cost adjusted by a price index which purports to reflect the change in cost of that type of asset between the date of acquisition and the balance sheet date. It is also a less prudent value than historic cost when prices are rising because it brings into account gains which are not realised and may never be realised.

5.  HOLMES, GEOFFREY, Replacement Value Accounting, *Accountancy*. March 1972, pp. 4–8.

Nevertheless the weight of the objections seems to be diminished by existing practice. Current values of fixed assets are already incorporated into accounts without causing exceptional audit problems, and the use of current replacement cost for stocks would be a relatively minor change except, perhaps, for those companies which value stock at marginal cost. When one takes into account the amount of arbitrary choice in present methods based on historic cost it seems that in many cases current value would be more objective because there is some sort of external standard with which it may be compared.

Another objection to the use of current values is that unrealised gains are recorded, but unrealised gains are already recognised in accounts when fixed assets are revalued, although they are excluded from the profit and loss account. It is permissible to bring into the profit and loss account unrealised gains on long term contracts and one company has been reported as bringing into account unrealised gains on quoted securities held as current assets.[6] If it is important to distinguish realised from unrealised gains it is a simple matter to separate them in the accounts, by dividing the profit and loss account into two stages. It is also worth recalling that the objection to the calculation of trading profits based on historic costs is that it overstates profits when prices are rising and that adjustment to a current cost basis would provide a more prudent estimate of profits.

### 3.7 Current Values and Profit Measurement
It must be accepted, however, that profit measurement is not automatically dealt with by using current values in the balance sheet. Profit is essentially the surplus which arises during a period; the amount which could be distributed and leave the capital invested unchanged. The problem is what is meant by maintaining capital unchanged. As Examples 2 and 3 show, maintaining the same capital in money terms is not the same as maintaining the same assets, or capital, in real terms. If current values at the beginning of the period are based on different prices than the current values at the end

---

6. *Accountancy Age*, 8 September 1972, p. 2 reported that Triumph Investment Trust included in the profit and loss account unrealised profits on securities amounting to one quarter of its total profits.

of the period then the increase in value may not be a real gain and
the profit will be inflated by the effects of price changes.

One answer to the problem is provided by matching current
costs with current revenues in the profit and loss account. If goods
held in stock increase in price they are revalued and the surplus, or
holding gain is transferred direct to reserve. When the goods are sold
or used the full current cost is charged as an expense. Similarly the
revaluation of fixed assets creates a surplus which is transferred to
reserve and depreciation is based on the current cost. If the company
continues to hold the same types and quantities of assets then it may
be argued that the holding gains are not real gains because they merely
reflect the higher prices of the assets held by the company. The real
improvement in capital, and therefore the real profit, is measured
by the profit and loss account. The real profit could be distributed
without disturbing the assets necessary to maintain the business at the
same size. On the other hand if the company anticipates price changes
and takes an advantage by building up stocks temporarily, part of
the holding gain is a speculative profit which is a real gain. Similarly,
if the company changes the composition and size of its asset holdings,
the question of what is a real gain and what is not becomes
obscure—for example if it is possible to sell the existing factory
building and move to another, which is just as convenient but only
half the price, how should the surplus on sale be dealt with?

It seems therefore that to deal with the problem of profit
measurement one must return to the definition of profit as an
increase in capital during a period and attempt to measure capital at
the beginning and the end of a period in terms of money units of the
same value or purchasing power. Even this does not provide a simple
solution because it is clear that the process depends on the point of view
from which profit is measured. What the company purchases is
not what the shareholder purchases and what one shareholder
purchases is not the same as the expenditure of another shareholder.
It is conceivable that the types of goods which a company buys are
stable in price and that the historic cost profit and loss account
provides a sound measure of real profit. The company has no need
of additional capital, profits are stable, and the whole profit is
distributed each year. If prices of goods bought by shareholders are

rising the constant dividend paid by the company buys less and less for the shareholder as the time passes. From his point of view it represents a falling profit and in addition the stable capital of the company is declining in value at the same time.

Although the problem of profit measurement appears to be very complicated and we must recognise that profit is a very crude concept, the use of current values in the balance sheet simplifies the problem to a considerable extent. Because all items in any balance sheet are in current terms, it is a simple matter for anyone to adjust the capital at the beginning of the year by the index of prices which he considers to be appropriate and so eliminate the effect of changing purchasing power of the money unit. The balance of profit represents real, consumable gain. If companies were to adjust opening capital by an agreed general price index this would provide a useful guide to shareholders, whilst maintaining the comparability of accounts. Any shareholder preferring a different index adjustment would be able to substitute his own figures with little calculation.

### 3.8 General Price Level Adjustments

One criticism of historic cost accounts is that they are mathematically incorrect in adding together monetary units which differ in value. To add together £1,000 spent on machinery in 1960 and another £1,000 spent in 1970 and call the result 'cost of machinery £2,000' is as much nonsense as adding 240 old pence and 240 new pence and calling the result 480 pence. The pence may be added by converting the old pence into equivalent new pence to give a correct sum of 340 new pence. Similarly if £1,000 in 1960 is regarded as having been equivalent in purchasing power to £1,500 in 1970 the total cost of machines may be expressed in terms of 1970 currency as £2,500. This does not imply that the machine bought in 1960 would cost £1,500 in 1970—it may cost more or less. The adjustment is not intended to value the machine but to value the pounds spent on the machine.

'In short, the object is not to ascertain the current cost or prospective replacement cost of particular assets. . . . It is to apply to investment by all types of businesses in all types of assets a common standard of measurement which will translate past investment at varying dates into its current monetary equivalent.'[7]

Once it is accepted that historic cost accounts need to take into account the effects of price changes, the adjustment for changes in the general purchasing power of money, or general price level adjustment, has the attractions of relative simplicity and objectivity. The resulting accounts are only one step removed from the historic cost accounts and, provided the same price index is used by all companies, the result is as objective and as verifiable by the auditor as the original accounts.

This solution to the problem of changing prices appears to have the support of a number of leading professional accountants. The method has been expounded in a paper prepared for the Research Foundation of the English Institute[7] and the Accounting Standards Steering Committee has issued a discussion paper and an Exposure Draft on the subject.[8] For published accounts it has been suggested that the aim of the adjustment should be to reveal to the shareholder information about his investment and earnings in terms of the average command over consumption goods. The Accounting Standards Steering Committee discussion paper has clearly accepted this in recommending the use of the Consumer Price Index, on the grounds that it covers the whole field of consumer expenditure, with the monthly Retail Price Index being used for short period adjustments. The historic cost accounts are still regarded as important, partly because many legal obligations are implicitly based on them, and the suggestion is that price level adjusted accounts should be issued as a supplement to, not instead of, the historic accounts.

Whilst the suggested adjustments go some way towards overcoming the problems of interpretation created by price changes, the result is

---

7. THE RESEARCH FOUNDATION OF THE INSTITUTE OF CHARTERED ACCOUNTANTS IN ENGLAND AND WALES, 'Accounting for Stewardship in a Period of Inflation', p. 9.

8. ACCOUNTING STANDARDS STEERING COMMITTEE, Inflation and Accounts, Reported in *Accountancy*, September 1971, pp. 496–506. Exposure Draft ED8, 'Accounting for Changes in the Purchasing Power of Money', was issued in January 1973.

a compromise which depends for its justification on the need for objectivity in published accounts. On balance it would seem to be a small step in the right direction and as such the initiative of the ASSC should be welcomed.

## 3.9 Price Indices

The validity of price level adjustments including both the use of a specific price index to calculate the current value of an asset and the adjustment of money values by means of a general price index, depends on our ability to measure price changes with reasonable accuracy. The construction of an index requires that the price of the same goods be found at two points of time, so that the price at one time may be expressed as a proportion of the price of the other. For example if the price index for butter changes from 100 to 120 it indicates that the quantity of butter which could be bought for 100 pence at the base date would cost 120 pence at the later date. Two problems have to be faced in constructing an index for a single good.

1.  At any one point in time a variety of prices may be charged for similar goods; official price lists may be only a starting point for negotiation and may not be a fair statement of prices actually paid. It is necessary in these circumstances to select a representative price, which may be the price paid in an actual transaction or the average of several transactions.

2.  Goods do not remain the same over time. Products change in quality, new products are introduced and old ones are discontinued. The process of comparing prices may involve the selection of similar products because identical products do not exist at two different points of time, and may require an allowance for the effect on the price of the differences between the products. If a television set is less likely to break down than an earlier model the prices cannot be compared without making allowances for the increased reliability.

A general price index traces the change in total cost of a selected parcel of goods over time. In addition to measuring the prices of the goods contained in the parcel the compiler of the index has two further problems to deal with.

1.　The goods have to be selected to accord with the spending habits or pattern of trading of the sector which is being represented. If a consumer price index is being constructed it is necessary to select a typical or average consumer and account for the goods which he buys. If one is interested in purchases made by the textile industry the choice will be determined by reference to a typical textile firm.

2.　The parcel of goods selected must be representative at more than one point in time. If spending patterns change then it may be necessary to decide the parcel of goods at one date which is equivalent to a different parcel at another date. When prices of different goods change at different rates the movement of the index may be affected materially by the proportions of the various goods incorporated in it. Table 3.1 illustrates the price changes which have occurred in the Retail Price Index over the period 1962 to 1972. Durable goods which make up 5.8% of the index rose in price by 39.1% in that period whilst housing which is 12.1% of the index rose by 88.8%. Each

*Table 3.1 General Index of Retail Prices (16 January 1962 = 100)*

| 18 April 1972 | Price Index | Weights |
|---|---|---|
| Food | 164.6 | 251 |
| Alcoholic drink | 157.8 | 66 |
| Tobacco | 138.4 | 53 |
| Housing | 188.8 | 121 |
| Fuel and light | 174.3 | 60 |
| Durable household goods | 139.1 | 58 |
| Clothing and footwear | 139.9 | 89 |
| Transport and vehicles | 153.3 | 139 |
| Miscellaneous goods | 166.8 | 65 |
| Services | 177.3 | 52 |
| Meals bought and consumed outside the home | 176.3 | 46 |
| All items | 161.8 | 1000 |

*Source:* CENTRAL STATISTICAL OFFICE, *Monthly Digest of Statistics,* May 1972. Table 172.

category is itself a general index made up of sub-groups. For example food includes tea, coffee and other beverages which rose 26% and fish which rose 91% over the period.

The construction of a price index for a single good is not an exact science but, like the art of accounting, involves a considerable amount of personal judgement. The compilation of a general price index draws even more on the skill and judgement of the statistician.

*3.10 Conversion of Foreign Currencies*

If a company carries on business in other countries, either through branches or through subsidiary companies, it is necessary to convert the accounts stated in foreign currencies into sterling in order to incorporate them into the published accounts. This procedure is analogous to that involved in dealing with changes in price level. When changes in exchange rates take place the question arises, what is the appropriate rate for conversion? Two methods have been adopted in practice and both are generally accepted.

(a)    The historic rate method in which the rate of exchange ruling at the date of the original transaction is used.

(b)    The closing rate method in which the rate of exchange ruling at the balance sheet date is used.

Broadly speaking a company may choose to use the closing rate method for all items, or it may restrict the closing rate method to current assets and current liabilities and convert other items at the historic rate, provided it uses the same method consistently.

For money, and obligations and rights expressed in money terms, the closing rate method is clearly the more realistic. In the case of fixed assets, on the other hand, the validity of the results depends on the relative price changes underlying the change in rates.

Consider an investment of 40,000 bingos in Bingoland when the exchange rate was 4 bingos to £1 and the sterling cost was £10,000. Subsequently the exchange rate changes to 5 bingos to £1. In the company's sterling accounts the investment may be expressed either as costing £10,000, at the historic exchange rate or £8,000 at the closing rate.

If prices in Bingoland have risen whilst United Kingdom prices have remained stable then the historic rate seems to be more appropriate, because it more nearly represents the current cost of a similar investment. If prices in the United Kingdom have fallen whilst in Bingoland prices have remained the same the closing rate method seems to be more suitable. If prices in both countries have changed neither method may clearly represent the position.

A satisfactory treatment of foreign investment demands, first, the adjustment of the accounts for price changes in the original currency and, second, conversion of the currency figures at the current rate of exchange. This assumes that the rates of exchange are not held at artificial levels for long periods and that no restrictions on conversion exist. Either of these factors may distort the picture and make it difficult to incorporate the foreign currency figures in the sterling accounts in a way which is not misleading.

### 3.11 Summary

Price changes tend to reduce the usefulness of accounts prepared on the basis of historic transactions but although this has been recognised for a considerable time there has been no concerted action to improve the accounts. Individual companies have modified historic costs, mainly by revaluing fixed assets from time to time. The revaluation is done at irregular intervals and in piecemeal fashion, so that some assets may be currently revalued whilst others remain at cost or an earlier valuation. Dissatisfaction with the result has led to interest in the possibility of creating an agreed procedure for adjusting accounts for price changes. The method which appears to be favoured is that of retaining the historic cost accounts but publishing supplementary statements in which the figures are converted to the current price level by means of a general price index. Whilst this is a compromise solution its adoption would be an improvement on the present confused situation.

# 4 Investments in Other Companies

'. . . Where a company conducts an important part of its business through the medium of other companies, whether more or less than 50 per cent owned, the mere disclosure of dividend income is unlikely to be sufficient to give shareholders adequate information regarding the sources of their income and of the manner in which their funds are being employed.'[1]

## 4.1 Investments in Equity

In the case of assets which are used up in the course of business it may be argued that historic cost provides a reasonable indication of position and profitability, provided prices are stable. In the case of investment in equity shares of other companies it is accepted that historic cost conceals vital information. The strict historic cost treatment of a holding of shares bought as an investment is:

1. Record the cost in the balance sheet whilst the shares are held, unless a permanent fall in value takes place, when the cost may be written down to the new value.
2. Record in the profit and loss account dividends received or receivable in the period; in other words income from investments is confined to dividends.
3. Record the excess of proceeds of sale over cost as a capital gain

1. INSTITUTE OF CHARTERED ACCOUNTANTS IN ENGLAND AND WALES, 'Statement of Standard Accounting Practice', M1, para 2.

and not as income. The gain may be transferred direct to
reserves, without passing through the profit and loss account.

In some cases the capital gain may be deducted from the cost
of remaining investments to reduce the amount of the net cost to the
company. The profit and loss account of the investing company does
not, therefore, record the full current earnings of the investment,
partly because all earnings are not distributed, and partly because,
when the increase in value is realised by sale, the surplus is separated
from annual trading results. The problem is magnified if the investing
company has a substantial influence on the affairs of the company
in which it has invested, so that it can determine what proportion
of profits should be retained. In such a case the existence of a
substantial pool of undistributed, and undisclosed, profits which could
be drawn upon at any time by the investing company would mean
that the declared profits of that company would be very largely under
the control of the directors. To quote a statement of the Institute of
Chartered Accountants:

> 'Where trade investments include an investment in a company
> which earns or has earned very substantial profits and accumulated
> large reserves, the amounts distributed by it in dividend being
> relatively insignificant, the long term value of the trade investments
> may be greatly in excess of the amount at which they are stated in
> the balance sheet. This excess would not be apparent from the
> balance sheet and would not normally be reflected elsewhere in
> the accounts because unlike a subsidiary the retained income would
> not be apparent from consolidated or group accounts. Some explanation
> may therefore be needed in these exceptional circumstances to
> enable the accounts to show a fair view.'[2]

If a company is engaged in the trade of buying and selling shares
then the shares held are trading stock, to be valued at cost or lower net
realisable value, and all profits on realisation are trading profits. The

2. INSTITUTE OF CHARTERED ACCOUNTANTS IN ENGLAND AND WALES,
   Recommendation N20, para 23. 'Trade investments' was an undefined term
   used in the Companies Act 1948 but abandoned in the 1967 Act.
   It referred approximately to the investments discussed later in the
   chapter as Investments in Associated Companies.

discussion which follows is confined to the treatment of long term investments for which, because they are held for long periods of time, the historic figures are especially deficient. In particular it deals with methods adopted to reveal the full earnings, including retained or undistributed profits, connected with the investment and to provide an indication of the value of the shareholdings.

*4.2 Subsidiary Companies and Consolidated Accounts*
Instead of holding assets and incurring liabilities directly, a company may operate through the intermediary of another company which it controls. It may for instance hold all the shares in that other company—its subsidiary company—so that for all practical purposes the two companies are one, or it may hold a lesser number but still control operations. A company is defined as a subsidiary of another 'if, but only if,—

(a)   that other either—
  (*i*)   is a member of it and controls the composition of its board of directors; or
  (*ii*)  holds more than half in nominal value of its equity share capital; or
(b)   the first-mentioned company is a subsidiary of any company which is that other's subsidiary.'[3]

In other words the relationship of holding company–subsidiary company occurs when the holding company holds shares in another company which it controls, usually because the shareholding is more than 50% of the equity. The relationship extends to a subsidiary of a subsidiary.

If the holding company issued only accounts drawn up on normal historic cost principles the use of subsidiary companies would be a method of concealing the true position of the organisation. The issue of separate accounts for each subsidiary might overcome the deficiency, although if the number of subsidiaries were large and the transactions between the companies extensive it would be difficult to obtain a clear view of the overall position. The remedy is to

3. Companies Act 1948. Section 154 (i).

treat the whole group of companies as a single entity and prepare
consolidated accounts, as a supplement to the accounts of the holding
company.

The nature of the consolidated balance sheet can be illustrated
by a simplified example.

*Example 1*

BALANCE SHEETS AT 31 DECEMBER 1972

|  | *Holding Co.* | *Subsidiary Co.* | *Consolidated* |
|---|---|---|---|
|  | *(£)* | *(£)* | *(£)* |
| Share capital | 1,000 | 300 | 1,000 |
| Reserves | 400 | 150 | 550 |
| Liabilities | 800 | 650 | 1,450 |
|  | 2,200 | 1,100 | 3,000 |
| Fixed assets | 1,000 | 600 | 1,600 |
| Shares in subsidiary Co. | 300 | | |
| Current assets | 900 | 500 | 1,400 |
|  | 2,200 | 1,100 | 3,000 |

In Example 1 the holding company holds all the shares in the
subsidiary company for which it subscribed at nominal value when
that company was formed. In the consolidation, the internal
relationship between the companies, represented by the share capital
in the subsidiary company's accounts and the purchase of those shares
in the holding company's accounts, is eliminated and the overall
position of the two companies together is represented by the sum of
the remaining figures in the separate balance sheets. Thus the share
capital of the group, shown in the consolidated balance sheet, is the
same as the share capital of the holding company because these are
the only shares held by external shareholders. Similarly liabilities

represent all external liabilities after the elimination of any indebtedness between group companies, and assets are all group assets other than internal indebtedness. The reserves of the group include both profits of the holding company and profits of the subsidiary company earned since the subsidiary company became part of the group—that is, all retained profits of the group. Because the group is regarded for this purpose as a single entity, any profits earned in transactions between group companies and not finally realised by the group through external sale will be eliminated by writing down assets in the consolidated balance sheet to their cost to the group.

If the holding company held only 200 shares in the subsidiary, then the other 100 together with the proportion of reserves attributable to those shares, would appear in the consolidated balance sheet as outside (or minority) shareholders in the group. Assuming the balance sheets are drawn up immediately after the purchase of the shares by the holding company the consolidation would appear as in Example 2.

*Example 2*

BALANCE SHEET AT 31 DECEMBER 1972

|  | *Holding Co.* (£) | *Subsidiary Co.* (£) | *Consolidated* (£) |
|---|---|---|---|
| Share capital | 1,000 | 300 | 1,000 |
| Reserves | 400 | 150 | 400 |
| Outside shareholders in subsidiary |  |  | 150 |
| Liabilities | 800 | 650 | 1,450 |
|  | 2,200 | 1,100 | 3,000 |
| Fixed assets | 1,000 | 600 | 1,600 |
| Shares in subsidiary Co. | 300 |  |  |
| Current assets | 900 | 500 | 1,400 |
|  | 2,200 | 1,100 | 3,000 |

The outside shareholders interest comprises shares (100) plus reserves (50) and is one-third of the equity capital of the subsidiary. The cost of the shares bought by the holding company is equal to the share of the net assets of the subsidiary represented by the nominal value of the shares (200) plus two-thirds of reserves at the date of acquisition (100), which are therefore eliminated from the consolidated balance sheet. If the cost had exceeded 300 the difference would be regarded as a payment for goodwill[4] and would appear as an asset of the group until written off. If the cost had been less than 300 the difference would be an addition to reserves of the group. The assets and liabilities of the group in Example 2 are the same as in Example 1. Thus the consolidated balance sheet is a statement of the assets, liabilities and capital of the group as a whole after eliminating any internal relationships between group companies. Group reserves do not include any of the subsidiary's reserves because they were earned before that company became a subsidiary.

A consolidated profit and loss account is drawn up in a similar manner to show the results of operations of the group as a single entity, after eliminating internal transactions such as transfers of goods between group companies, or payment of dividends by one group company to another. If there are minority shareholders in subsidiary companies their interest in the profit of the subsidiaries is stated as a deduction from the group profit to leave the net amount attributable to the holding company. It is not usual for a holding company to publish its own profit and loss account as well as a consolidated profit and loss account. The Companies Act 1948 section 149 (5) expressly approves the use of a single consolidated account provided it states separately the amount of the consolidated profit or loss which is dealt with in the holding company's own accounts—that is, the group profit attributable to holding company must be divided between that part which is contained in the holding companies profit and loss account, which is strictly the company's profit on historic cost principles

---

4. If the value of the assets of the subsidiary at the date of acquisition materially differs from book values then those assets may be restated at their new cost to the group, in which case the goodwill valuation is made by reference to the revalued assets.

and that which is retained in the subisdiary companies' accounts. In contrast the company will publish both its own and the consolidated balance sheet. If a flow of funds statement is prepared it will invariably be a group statement.

### 4.3 Investments Acquired in Exchange for an Issue of Shares

If an asset is acquired for a consideration other than cash the cost of the asset may not be clearly defined. In particular, if the purchase price is satisfied by the issue of shares in the company buying the asset, the cost may be regarded as the nominal value of the shares issued or the market value at the time of issue. The nominal value is the minimum amount at which the issue of new shares may be made without special dispensation of the Court and may therefore be properly regarded as the historic cost of the consideration. Market value, whilst providing a more reasonable statement of the transaction, appears to introduce a concept of opportunity cost or current value not generally applied in accounting statements. Nevertheless, both interpretations are found in practice and both command substantial support. As an example in 1963 the City of London Real Property Co. Ltd, which owned 51% of the shares in City and Victoria Property Co. Ltd, acquired the remaining 49% to increase their holding to 100%. In return, City of London issued 170,600 £1 shares, thus increasing its capital by this amount. The directors wished to treat the £170,600 as the cost of the additional investment in City and Victoria and obtained legal advice supporting this method. The auditors, on the other hand contended that as the market value of the 170,600 shares at the time of issue was £580,040 the accounts would not show a true and fair view of the company unless the cost of the investment was recorded as £580,040. Although the auditors view was allowed to prevail in this instance there is little doubt that a different auditor might have adopted the company's viewpoint.[5]

The Institute of Chartered Accountants' Recommendation on Treatment of Investments states:

5. The City of London Real Property Case, *Accountancy*, September 1964, pp. 773–78.

'Where . . . the consideration to a third party for the acquisition of an interest in a subsidiary is the issue of fully-paid shares in the holding company, the cost of the interest thus acquired is the value properly attributable to the shares of the holding company issued in exchange; this is not necessarily their nominal value.'[6]

The exposure draft on Accounting for Acquisitions and Mergers[7] states

'There is legal opinion to support the propriety in law of the practice of recording in the books of the holding company, at the nominal value of the shares issued, shares received by the holding company in exchange for shares issued.'

The statement suggests that this method should be restricted to accounting for mergers which is discussed in section 4.4.

The method adopted affects not only the amount at which the asset is recorded in the company's balance sheet, but also the profits of the company. By way of illustration assume that City of London had resold the shares in City and Victoria for £580,040 shortly after it had acquired them (in fact it did not) and consider the results shown by the two methods. In the method finally adopted by City of London the cost of shares was made up of £170,600 share capital and £409,440 share premium both of which represent subscribed capital which is not distributable by way of dividend. The only effect of the sale would have been in the balance sheet where the investment would have been replaced by the cash realised. If the cost of the shares had been recorded as £170,600 the £409,440 excess of sale price over the book value would have been recorded as a profit on sale and would have added to the amount available for distribution as dividends. The danger of recording the cost of assets at the nominal value of shares allotted in exchange is that a misleading impression may be given of the profitability of the company. The company may be able to convert

6. INSTITUTE OF CHARTERED ACCOUNTANTS IN ENGLAND AND WALES, 'Recommendations on Accounting Principles', N20. para 12.

7. ACCOUNTING STANDARDS STEERING COMMITTEE, Exposure Draft No. 3, Accounting for Acquisitions and Mergers (1971), para 25. Reprinted in *Accountancy*, February 1971 pp. 97–99.

what is really subscribed capital into realised profits and to pay
dividends out of those profits, so making the company appear much
more prosperous than it really is, at least for a time.

If the asset acquired consists of shares in another company
it may not be necessary to sell the shares in order to realise a profit.
All that is necessary is that substantial dividends be received from
that investment, either out of profits earned before the acquisition, or
out of profits realised by selling assets, which were recorded at values
much lower than current values at the date of acquisition. Provided
the distribution of dividends does not reduce the value of the
investment permanently below its recorded cost the amount so
realised adds to the profit of the investing company. If the other
company is a subsidiary company, or an associated company the total
profits of the group will be revealed by the consolidated accounts and
the drawing on reserves is not likely to mislead. There still remains,
however, the possibility of realising profits by the sale of the
subsidiary's assets which are stated at figures below their real cost of
acquisition to the group.

*4.4 Mergers*
The acquisition of shares in a subsidiary company may be interpreted
in one of two ways. It may be regarded as a purchase, in which the
ownership of the company changes, and this is clearly appropriate
when payment is made in cash. The full value of the transaction is
recorded in the accounts and the consolidation is as described in
section 4.2. If, on the other hand, payment is made by issuing shares
in the holding company to the shareholders of the subsidiary company,
the transaction may be regarded as a merger, or pooling of interests,
of two groups of shareholders. There has been no change in the
ownership of the companies and the assets should continue to be
recorded at their historic cost to the group. More important, perhaps,
the accounts should continue to show all undistributed profits of the
two companies as available for distribution and the pre-acquisition
profits of the subsidiary should not be eliminated in the consolidated
balance sheet. This result can be achieved if the holding company
records the purchase of the subsidiary company at the nominal value
of the shares issued in satisfaction of the purchase price.

The modified consolidation of the accounts may be illustrated
by re-interpreting Example 1. Assume that the accounts were drawn
up immediately after the acquisition of the subsidiary, in exchange
for 300 £1 shares in the holding company and that this
transaction has been recorded at the nominal value of those shares.
Then, although the reserves of the subsidiary are pre-acquisition
profits the consolidated balance sheet in Example 1 is a correct
statement of the merger. If the nominal value of the shares issued
had been greater than £300 the reserves would have been reduced
by the excess; if the nominal value had been less than £300 reserves
would have been increased but the difference would be segregated as
undistributable. As far as possible, within the law, the pre-acquisition
profits of the subsidiary company are preserved.

It has been recognised that merger accounting may be abused,
by companies buying profits and using them to inflate their dividends.
On the other hand, it is accepted that to prevent its use altogether
might impose hardship in genuine mergers if profits were to fall
drastically immediately after the merger when there were no reserves
from which a dividend could be paid. This has led to suggestions that
the use of this method should be restricted, although no action has
yet been taken. The Jenkins Committee recommended[8] that the right
of a holding company to distribute to its shareholders the pre-acquisition
profits of a subsidiary should be restricted, in the main, to cases where
a new company is formed to acquire at least 90% of the equity
shares of other companies in exchange for its own shares issued at a
premium, and that the profits of only one of the acquired companies
should be distributable. The recommendation was not incorporated
in the 1967 Companies Act. In 1971 The Accounting Standards
Steering Committee issued an Exposure Draft in which it was proposed
that a company should not be allowed a free choice but that the
method of treatment of the acquisition of a subsidiary should be
determined by the conditions. If it is identified as a merger the
purchase should be recorded in the holding company's balance sheet
at the nominal value of the shares issued and the consolidated balance

8. REPORT OF THE COMPANY LAW COMMITTEE 1962, H.M.S.O. Cmnd 1749
   para 350.

sheet should include pre-acquisition profits of the subsidiary. In all other cases the purchase should be recorded at the fair value of the shares or other consideration and the consolidation should exclude pre-acquisition profits of the subsidiary. The definition of a merger adopted by the Exposure Draft required that the following conditions be met:

'(a) the substance of the main businesses of the constituent companies continues in the amalgamated undertaking; and
(b) the equity voting rights of the amalgamated undertaking to be held by the shareholders of any one of the constituent companies is not more than three times the equity voting rights to be held by the shareholders of any of the other constituent companies; and
(c) the amalgamation results from an offer to equity voting shareholders and not less than 90 per cent in value of the offer is in the form of equity voting capital with rights identical with the equity voting capital rights of the offeree company or companies already in issue; for this purpose convertible loan stock or equity voting capital which can be converted into cash through an underwriting agreement is not to be regarded as equity voting capital; and
(d) the offer is approved by the voting shareholders of the company making the offer and it is accepted by shareholders representing at least 90 per cent of the total equity capital (voting and non-voting) of the company or companies receiving the offer.'[9]

At the time of writing no Statement of Standard Practice has emerged and there is obviously difficulty in obtaining agreement on this subject.

### 4.5 Associated Companies

The relationship between companies may fall short of that between holding and subsidiary companies and still involve a substantial amount of influence by the investing company in the affairs of the other. The term 'associated company' has been defined by the Institute of Chartered Accountants as follows:

9. ACCOUNTING STANDARDS STEERING COMMITTEE, Exposure Draft No. 3, 'Accounting for Acquisitions and Mergers' (1971), para 7.

'A company (not being a subsidiary of the investing group or company) is an associated company of the investing group or company if
  (a) the investing group or company's interest in the associated company is that of a partner in a joint venture or consortium or
  (b) the investing group of company's interests in the associated company is for the long term and is substantial (i.e. not less than 20 per cent of the equity voting rights), and, having regard to the disposition of the other shareholdings, the investing group or company is in a position to exercise a significant influence over the associated company. In both cases it is essential that the investing group or company participates (usually through representation on the board) in commercial and financial policy decisions of the associated company, including the distribution of profits.'[10]

In order to provide a fuller statement of the trading results a number of companies with interests in associated companies have adopted the practice of bringing into the profit and loss account their full share of the associated company profits whether received as dividend or retained in the associated company. In contrast to the consolidation of subsidiary companies the amount is brought in as investment income—there is no consolidation of sales and expenses of associates—and is limited to the investing company's share of profit. There is no consolidation of balance sheet figures; the retained earnings of the associated company brought into the profit of the investing company are either added to the cost of the investment or deducted from the balance of profits carried forward. In the latter case the profit and loss account shows the full profits of the company and its associated companies but the balance sheet reverts to a strict historic cost basis, in which only dividends received or receivable are taken into account.

The practice of bringing undistributed profits of associated companies into the accounts of the investing company has been approved by professional accounting bodies and made obligatory for members of those bodies taking responsibility for company accounts. A distinction is drawn between a company's own accounts and the

10. INSTITUTE OF CHARTERED ACCOUNTANTS IN ENGLAND AND WALES, 'Statement of Standard Accounting Practice', M1 (1971), para 6.

consolidated accounts, which it prepares as a holding company having subsidiaries. In the company's own accounts only distributed profits of associated companies should be included.

> 'The view is taken that the inclusion of undistributed profits would ignore the separate legal entities of the companies concerned and, as regards the investing company, be in breach of the principle that credit should not be taken for investment income until it is received or receivable.'[11]

The profit of the investing company is therefore restricted to what is actually realised and distributable to shareholders. In the group consolidated accounts the full profitability is revealed by bringing into profit and loss account the group's share of profits (less losses) of associated companies, showing both profits before taxation and the tax on those profits. In the balance sheet the share of undistributed profit is added to the cost of the investment and indicates the increase in net assets of the associated companies since the investment was was made. In most cases therefore the published accounts will show investments in associated companies on two different bases; at historic cost in the company's own accounts and increased by undistributed profits in the consolidated accounts. If a company does not prepare consolidated accounts (e.g. if it has no subsidiaries) the company's own accounts will be adapted to show the information in the most convenient way, including the use of notes.

### 4.6 Other Investments

Although the treatment of subsidiary and associated companies has improved the information available to shareholders there remains the question of dealing with other investment in equity shares. In some companies, such as investment trusts, such shares may comprise a large proportion of the assets. Two main alternatives are found in use:

1.   The historic cost method described at the beginning of this chapter. The published accounts will contain notes to supplement

---

11. INSTITUTE OF CHARTERED ACCOUNTANTS IN ENGLAND AND WALES, 'Statement of Standard Accounting Practice', M1 (1971), para 1.

the historic cost data, indicating current market values or earnings of the shares.

2.    Revaluation, usually at market value at the date of the balance sheet. Market value may be the stock exchange quoted price (the middle market price) or the directors valuation. The use of market value by investment trusts has been supported by the English Institute of Chartered Accountants,[12] and for all companies, in a research study published by the Scottish Institute of Chartered Accountants.[13]

The sample of companies used in the Survey of Published Accounts indicates that the use of the market value is not common. Out of 233 instances in which quoted investments appeared in accounts, only 20 reported a balance sheet value equal to market value in 1970–71. Of the remainder, there were 147 reports of market value in excess of balance sheet value and 66 cases in which market value was less than the balance sheet value.[14] The survey is limited to commercial and industrial companies and does not include investment trusts and other financial companies.

*4.7 Summary*

Historic cost is least satisfactory in providing a fair representation of the position and profitability of a company when dealing with assets which normally grow in value. This deficiency is especially evident when a company invests in equity shares of other companies. A study of the methods of dealing with such investments reveals a continuing attempt to overcome the defects of historic cost whilst remaining within the historic cost framework. This has entailed the provision of supplementary statements—notably consolidated accounts, treating a group of companies as if it were a single company, and also the use of notes of current market values. Payment for an asset by issuing a

12.  INSTITUTE OF CHARTERED ACCOUNTANTS IN ENGLAND AND WALES, 'Recommendation on Accounting Principles', N28, para 10.
13.  INSTITUTE OF CHARTERED ACCOUNTANTS OF SCOTLAND, Research Study. Balance Sheets of Investment Trust Companies, *Accountants Magazine*, November 1969, p. 602.
14.  INSTITUTE OF CHARTERED ACCOUNTANTS IN ENGLAND AND WALES, 'Survey of Published Accounts 1970–71', p. 95.

company's own shares in exchange, combined with a strict historic cost interpretation, may seriously understate the real cost of the asset in the company's balance sheet, and permit the conversion of subscribed capital into realised profits. This is particularly a problem in company mergers and attempts are being made to restrict the use of merger accounting to appropriate cases.

# 5 The Form and Content of Accounts

*'When we speak or write about anything we can only say a finite number of things about it. We cannot describe and convey ideas with infinitesimal precision: we cannot classify or pin-point with absolute accuracy but must always be content to do so within some arbitrary limits of practical utility.'*[1]

## 5.1 Introduction

Although the choice of the balance sheet and profit and loss account as the main vehicles for conveying financial information has a strong influence on the type of data reported and the way in which it is reported, there is still considerable room for choice in the amount of detail which is given and the form of presentation. The amount of detail contained in published accounts has increased over the years, stimulated by the demands of investors and others and reinforced by the changes in company law, and this in turn has led companies to seek better ways of setting out the data so that it is easier to read and understand.

Financial accounts form a collection of data about a company. If too much data is given it will be useless except to those prepared to spend considerable time and effort in extracting relevant summaries; if too little is provided then important aspects will be concealed. For example, if it could be arranged that shareholders had access to all

1. CHERRY, COLIN, 'On Human Communication', 2nd Edition, M.I.T. Press, 1966, p. 88.

books and records of the company few would find any benefit in the privilege. It would still be necessary to extract those items which were regarded as of value and this would involve classification and summarisation. On the other hand an annual report which consisted of nothing more than the profit of the year would be of little value. The accounts are therefore a compromise and reflect a judgement of what is relevant or material to the understanding of the financial affairs of the company.

The selection of appropriate data is not made easier by the fact that the purposes to be served by the accounts are only identified in very broad terms. Those who supply capital to the company want to know what is being done with it and what results are being achieved. The ability of a company to pay its creditors on time needs to be demonstrated. It is desirable to know whether a company is profitable or not. Shareholders would like information which would help to establish the value of their shares. Economists demand data which is useful in their studies of business. One can identify many purposes which can be served by financial data, and many in which the financial data plays only a part in a much more extensive investigation. The attempt to serve such a variety of needs means the publication of a considerable amount of data and imposes a burden of selection which is very great.

*5.2 The Concept of Materiality*
The question of what is material information is a difficult one but it lies at the heart of financial reporting. The concept of materiality has been described as

> '. . . part of the wisdom of life. Its basic meaning is that there
> is no need to be concerned with what is not important or with
> what does not matter. Man's work is burdensome enough
> without the need to pay attention to trivia.'[2]

The American Accounting Association described materiality as

> '. . . a state of relative importance. The materiality of an item
> may depend on its size, its nature or a combination of both.

2. BERNSTEIN, L A, The Concept of Materiality, *The Accounting Review* January 1967, p. 87.

An item should be regarded as material if there is reason
to believe that knowledge of it would influence the decision of
an informed investor.'[3]

Decisions about what is material have to be made at every stage
in the construction of accounts. In the absence of legal requirements,
a balance sheet could consist of two figures, which would be
identical—net assets and capital—or, at the other extreme, it could
list each asset and liability separately. There is a clear advantage in
having the cash in hand reported separately from the investment in
plant and machinery, because they have such different effects on the
financial position. Whether one is concerned with the ability of a
company to pay its creditors as they fall due, with the amount likely
to be realised on winding up the company, or with the ability to earn
profits, the difference between cash and plant is material. On the
other hand, in most cases there is no significant gain in information
from the listing of each debtor by name; indeed the volume of data
which this would entail would probably reduce the clarity of the
statements. If there are several bank balances it may be reasonable
to merge them into a single total or it may be important to
distinguish those accounts in credit from those which are overdrawn.
It is generally accepted that profits and losses from the normal trading
operations of a company should be distinguished from unusual items
such as those arising on the sale of fixed assets, and that even in
reporting the results of normal operations it may be necessary to draw
attention to items which have had an abnormal effect on those
results. In particular it is recognised that the effects of a change in
the basis of accounting should be reported unless the amount is
insignificant. In the accounts as a whole a decision has to be made
as to the degree of approximation which is satisfactory. Few companies
now report figures which include pence and many round off the
figures to the nearest thousand pounds, because the simplification
makes for ease of reading without reducing the information given to a
significant extent.
        The question of what is material extends to all aspects of the

---

3. A A A COMMITTEE ON CONCEPTS AND STANDARDS UNDERLYING CORPORATE
    FINANCIAL STATEMENTS, *Accounting Review*, October 1957, p. 543.

accounts and calls for continuous exercise of judgement on the part
of those responsible for them. There is a large number of items which
the Companies Acts specifically state must be shown, and for those
items the judgement as to what is material has already been made.
In some cases, such as the disclosure of sums payable for the hire of
plant and machinery, the requirement to disclose is made subject
to the judgement of the directors as to whether the amount is material,
but in most cases no discretion is given. Nevertheless it is not sufficient
to restrict the information given to the specific requirements of the Acts,
although the philosophy behind those requirements must influence
directors in deciding what they should disclose. The Jenkins Report
made it clear that the Acts could not give an exhaustive list of the
information necessary to give a true and fair view in all circumstances.

> 'Whether the information provided in the accounts is enough
> to give a true and fair view is to some extent a matter of the
> opinion of the directors based on the circumstances of the
> particular company. In the last resort the auditor must decide
> whether he is prepared to state that in his opinion the accounts
> give a true and fair view;. . .'[4]

In making his decision the auditor must be guided by experience
rather than precise rules and definitions.

> 'The interpretation of what is "material" is a matter of the
> exercise of professional judgement based on experience and
> the requirement to give a true and fair view.'[5]

The reason for the lack of guidance is to be found in the complexity
of the decision. Even if it is accepted that accounts are to be simply
summaries of historical data there are at least three aspects of the
question as to what is material:

1.    The difference in quality between items which will determine
       whether they are to be classified together or not. The significance

4. Report of the Company Law Committee (1962), H.M.S.O. Cmnd 1749,
   para 334.
5. INSTITUTE OF CHARTERED ACCOUNTANTS IN ENGLAND AND WALES,
   The Interpretation of 'Material' in Relation to Accounts (1968), para 4.

of the classification is related to the purpose of the information and, as the purpose of accounts is not well defined, one cannot expect to find precise rules of classification.

2.   The size of an item. An unusual type of adjustment of £1,000 to the profit of a company earning £5,000 a year is significant but to a company earning £5 million a year it would not be noticed. Materiality is not necessarily related to profit but may be assessed in connection with other characteristics such as total assets or the amount of directors' emoluments. It is also possible that whilst one item on its own is not material the cumulative effect of several items may be very significant.

3.   The cost of providing the data compared with the benefit of receiving it. The expected benefit to the shareholder of being able to make a better assessment of the value of his shares, or the risk of failure of the firm, must be compared with the cost of providing and processing the data. If the cost exceeds the benefit then the company is not justified in providing it. Material information in this sense is that which has a net value to the user.

In order to define what is material it would be necessary to identify the decision processes in which an item is used and test the sensitivity of the decisions to changes in the item. If, for example, it were found that the only determinant of share values was the current earnings figure then one would expect small errors in earnings (or small extra-ordinary items of profit or loss) to be material. If, on the other hand, the influence of earnings was small then relatively large errors may not be material. Obviously if earnings were disregarded altogether then, for that purpose, the earnings figure is not material. In the absence of much greater knowledge of the ways in which decisions are made it is unlikely that a useful definition of what is material will be obtained in this way and in practice we must be satisfied with something much more subjective. One approach might be to attempt to obtain a consensus of expert opinion on the factors which are of importance in financial reports and the amount of tolerance which should be allowed in estimating the figures. Thus if it is agreed that stock valuation is a highly significant figure the limits of accuracy of measurement would be laid down by an authoritative body. As auditors must continually be called upon to make such judgements in the course of their verification of the accounts, such a course should not be impossible. In the meantime, however, we have a situation in which personal judgement must be made without any formal guidance and this provides another source of variety in accounting which can lead to lack of comparability between companies. For example, an examination of the treatment of extra-ordinary gains and losses by United States companies led to the comment that

> '. . . practice is so diffused that the size of an item in relation
> to net income appears hardly to have any important effect' and
> '. . . viewing practice as a whole, there emerges no pattern which
> would suggest that there are any agreed-upon criteria regarding
> the application of the concept of materiality.'[6]

*5.3 The Form of Accounts*

The form in which accounts are presented can make a big difference to the understanding of the financial situation. The more data there is to be presented the greater is the need for clear layout of the statements. One way of concealing significant information is to publish a large quantity of data but present it in such a higgledy-piggledy fashion that it is difficult to distinguish what is important from what is trivial. The balance sheet and the profit and loss account have been improved over the years as the volume of information given has increased. In the 1930's a balance sheet consisted generally of a list of assets on one side and a list of liabilities and capital on the other. In a modern balance sheet there is an attempt to direct attention to the most important aspects of the situation by appropriate layout, by grouping similar items under headings such as fixed assets and current assets, be relegating much of the detail to notes and by incorporating comparative figures to reveal the main changes which have taken place. As more information is given about the revenues and expenses,

6. BERNSTEIN, LEOPOLD A, The Concept of Materiality, *The Accounting Review*, January 1967, pp. 86–95. Bernstein gives an example of one company which included in income a profit on fixed assets amounting to 26% of net income, whilst another company transferred to retained earnings a similar profit amounting to 3% of net income.

and profits and losses, the form of the profit and loss account and the
methods of disclosing exceptional items become important. The flow
of funds statement which is an alternative way of presenting the data
to show the main financial changes during a period is now being
published by an increasing number of companies, and it is now fairly
common for some of the more important figures such as profit and
capital employed to be extracted and displayed in summaries covering
periods of up to 10 and sometimes more years. Thus the growth in the
amount of information provided by companies has been accompanied
by attempts to set out the very complicated statements in a more
informative manner.

*5.4 Extra-ordinary Items of Profit and Loss*
One problem in the design of accounts which has been widely
debated is that of reporting profits and losses other than those which
are regarded as arising from the normal operations of the business.
Both ordinary profit and extra-ordinary items ultimately affect the
balance sheet in the same way by increasing or reducing reserves,
and it is accepted that extra-ordinary items should be separately
reported, so the question is simply in what form the detailed data
should be displayed. On the one hand there are those who prefer the
profit and loss account to be confined to a statement of the profits
from normal recurring business operations, and all other items to be
adjusted directly in the reserves. On the other hand it is argued that
this method may lead many readers to overlook such items and that a
clear account of all profits and losses should be contained in the profit
and loss account. If a company publishes a summary of the main
financial figures for a period of several years the treatment of extra-
ordinary items in that summary is of special importance because the
reader may not have ready access to the detailed notes on the original
accounts. The Accounting Standards Steering Committee has issued two
exposure drafts on this subject and it seems likely that the latter view
will prevail. If this happens the profit and loss account will show two
stages in the profit calculation, the profit from normal operations and
the profit after adjusting extra-ordinary items. For this purpose unusual
items which arise from the normal activities of the business, such as,
exceptional bad debt charges, abnormal writing off of stocks or

fluctuations in foreign exchange have been distinguished from
extra-ordinary items such as profits and losses arising from a
discontinuance of a significant part of the business, the sale of long
term investments, writing off goodwill and major realignments of
currencies. Whilst both types of item may call for separate disclosure
it has been suggested that those connected with normal trading should
be adjusted in the calculation of profit whilst extra-ordinary items
should be adjusted after the normal profit has been calculated.

One example of this type of problem is found in the accounts
of Pye of Cambridge Ltd for the year 1966.[7] The profit and loss account
revealed a loss after tax and minority interests of £1,239,000.
The appropriation account also listed, amongst other items, net losses
attributable to prior years £1,189,000 and provision for losses on
reorganisation £1,500,000. Turning to the notes on the capital reserve
one finds a surplus on disposal of investments £3,611,000 less amounts
written off other investments £2,168,000, surpluses arising on
revaluation of properties £4,137,000 and goodwill written off £1,390,000.
Whether this was the best way to show the considerable changes which
arose in the reorganisation of the company, which took place at that
time, is a matter of opinion, but it is clear that only a careful reading
of the full accounts and notes would reveal the major changes which
took place.

Another example which is worth quoting is that of S and K
Holdings Ltd, which reported in 1971 a profit after tax and minority
interests of £488,000 less exceptional items of £112,000, these two
figures being incorporated in the ten year summary included in the
annual report. The exceptional items included consulting fees,
compensation for loss of office and other non-recurring items. Notes on
the reserves listed other items, including provisions for repairs, writing
down of current assets and losses and expenses on reorganisation and
disposal of parts of the business amounting to £846,000. In the words
of Geoffrey Holmes who reviewed the accounts,

'It is difficult for an outsider to appreciate just why the £846,000
has been charged to reserve, whereas the £112,000 net in respect of

7. The accounts of Pye are discussed in *Accountancy*, December 1966,
   pp. 883–8.

consultancy fees, compensation for loss of office and other non-recurring charges has been charged "below the line" in the profit and loss account.'[8]

The importance of the topic may be judged from the discussion of exceptional, non-recurring and prior year items in the Survey of Published Accounts.[9] In the accounts of 300 companies surveyed in 1970–71 there were no less than 1,716 such items ranging from currency revaluation to investment grants, of which 1,111 were adjusted in the reserves and 605 adjusted at various stages of the profit and loss account. Whilst many of these would probably be relatively small the effect of such adjustments in any individual company cannot be ignored.

*5.5 Summary*

The art of accounting is that of choosing relevant information about the financial position of a company and displaying it in the most informative way. Questions as to content and form have to be decided at every stage and include not only the design of the traditional financial statements such as the balance sheet and the profit and loss account but also such matters as the best position for the auditors' report to ensure that it is seen, and the design and content of supplementary statements such as statistical summaries. The task of portraying the financial affairs of a complex entity such as a company which may be operating in several industries and in different countries is clearly no small one. The discussion of the financial statements has revealed the possibility of great variety in form, content and methods of placing money values on the items contained in the reports. The variety of treatment has been the subject of much debate and it is possible to take different views of the best way to obtain informative accounts.

8. The accounts of S and K Holdings Ltd are discussed by Geoffrey Holmes, Points from Published Accounts, *Accountancy*, August 1971, pp. 464–8.
9. THE GENERAL EDUCATIONAL TRUST OF THE INSTITUTE OF CHARTERED ACCOUNTANTS IN ENGLAND AND WALES, Survey of Published Accounts, 1970–71, pp. 58–64.

One alternative is for regulations to be drawn up specifying a standard form of accounts and the methods to be used in arriving at the amounts to be entered in the forms. The proposals of the Commission of European Communities for harmonising company law in the Common Market include a prescribed format of accounts. If the proposals are adopted they will ensure a high degree of comparability but at the expense of squeezing a variety of organisations into one form which must be sufficiently general to cater for all businesses. There is an added disadvantage, that if the development of accounting reports must await legislation there is a strong probability that little or no development will take place and the prescribed form may rapidly become misleading as new business methods are used. Even without the drag of legislation, accounting has been slow to deal with such matters as the development of leasing and the effects of inflation.

Another approach is to accept that some variety is necessary to deal with different business situations and to specify only those items which are regarded as essential, within a general obligation to disclose anything which materially affects the understanding of the position. This view has tended to be adopted in Britain, where there is no prescribed form of accounts but the Companies Acts impose a dual obligation on directors, first to give a true and fair view of the state of affairs and profit and second to publish at least the information specified in detail in the Acts. As the Jenkins Committee commented compliance with the detailed provisions does not necessarily result in a true and fair view and it would be difficult, if not impossible to prescribe regulations which would produce a true and fair view in all circumstances. Thus the judgement of the directors and the auditors must, in the final outcome decide the issue. As has been demonstrated this approach tends to produce a wide variety of methods, which are not necessarily justified by different circumstances.

Ideally a system of regulation should be sufficiently flexible to allow appropriate variety and not discourage the development of better methods of reporting, whilst reducing to a minimum unnecessary proliferation of methods. The EEC Accountants Study Group consisting of representatives of accounting bodies in 10 countries has accepted the need for some flexibility in accounting statements. In commenting on the proposals of the European Commission it has suggested that

'Annual accounts should be required to show a true and fair view of the results and financial position of a company' and that 'Departure from the prescribed format should be obligatory if fair presentation demands it. . .'[10]

In Britain, professional accounting bodies have influenced the way in which accounting statements have been drawn up, both by informal recommendations issued for guidance, and more recently by establishing standards with which their members are expected to comply. This aspect of accounts is reviewed in the next chapter.

10. *Accountancy*, August 1972, p. 8.

# 6 Professional Standards and the Stock Exchange

*'. . . those who measure, measure what they are able to measure and modify their definitions and theories accordingly.'* [1]

## 6.1 Introduction

The history of company accounts in this century has been one of gradual development as companies and accountants have sought to improve the information available to shareholders and others, reinforced by regulations of the Stock Exchange and legislation designed to create minimum standards of disclosure of financial information and bring all companies into line with the best practice of the time.

The aim of this chapter is to summarise the influence of the accounting profession and the Stock Exchange on published accounts.

A significant part has been played in developing accounting standards by the professional accounting bodies the work of which has been divided into two distinct stages:

1.  An advisory and codification stage in which the best existing practice has been disseminated and encouraged without attempting to choose a single best method.
2.  A more recent standard setting stage in which a conscious effort is being made to narrow the choice of method available

1. DEVINE, C T, Some Conceptual Problems in Accounting Measurements, in 'Research in Accounting Measurement', Ed. JAEDICKE, R K, *et al.*, American Accounting Association, 1966, p. 14.

and to impose sanctions in the event of failure to observe the
rules. Thus the present state might be described as moving
towards more precise formulation of rules for specified aspects
of the accounts within a general obligation to show a true
and fair view.

*6.2 Recommendations on Accounting Principles*
A dominant place must be given in the first stage to the
recommendations of the Institute of Chartered Accountants in England
and Wales. The English Institute began in 1942 to make
recommendations to members and a series of 29 statements, some
of which were replacements of earlier statements, was issued, the
latest being dated 1969. In addition to the formal recommendations
of the Council of the Institute technical notes have also been issued
on such matters as 'Consolidated Accounts', 'Terms Used in Published
Accounts', 'The Interpretation of "Material" ' and 'The Financial
and Accounting Responsibility of Directors'. Other accounting bodies
have avoided issuing formal recommendations on the grounds that
progress might be prevented by rigid adherence to rules, but a number
of useful research reports have been issued. The recommendations of
the English Institute, which have had wide influence, have generally
reported on and codified the best practice of the time. The statements
are not mandatory; they are issued for guidance and in most cases
suggest alternative methods. The Recommendation on the treatment
of Stock in Trade is drawn so as to allow either a full cost or a
marginal cost basis of valuation, or in special cases any other basis,
including selling price, which has acquired respectability by long use.
The recommendation on 'Depreciation of Fixed Assets' suggests that
the straight line basis should normally be adopted and appears to have
been generally followed, but a minority of companies has continued to
use the reducing balance and other methods. The 'Recommendations
on Rising Price Levels' suggest that in general fixed assets should not
be written up on the basis of replacement costs, but this recommendation
seems to have been widely disregarded. The historic cost basis has
been firmly supported throughout the recommendations except in the
case of investments held by investment companies in which case
current market value is recommended as an alternative to historic cost.

The Institutes have not always been in full agreement and a research study issued by the Scottish Institute of Chartered Accountants firmly supported current market value for investments to the exclusion of historic cost.[2]

Although they have been influential in improving the standard of published accounts the 'Recommendations on Accounting Principles' were not designed to bring about uniformity of method as between different companies and they did not do so. There were not only considerable differences between companies but the nature and effect of those differences were in many cases not detectable from the accounts. The events of the 1960's created increasing disillusion with financial reports and it was clear that something had to be done to improve the situation. One case in particular stands out. In 1967 GEC proposed to take over AEI and in the course of events the directors of AEI issued to shareholders a forecast of the profits of the current year. The forecast of £10 million was made after 10 months of the year had elapsed, on the basis of budgets which had been reliable in the past, and with the benefit of monthly accounts showing the results achieved to date. The takeover was successfully accomplished and GEC subsequently reported that AEI had incurred a loss for the year 1967 amounting to £4.5 million, a shortfall of £14.5 million compared with the forecast. Of this amount, £4.3 million was attributed to amounts written off stocks, £4.4 million to provisions for estimated losses on contracts, and £3.4 million to under-estimates of the cost of sales, together with other smaller adjustments. Whilst the precise reasons for the very large difference were not fully explained, it was generally agreed that a substantial part could be attributed to the lack of precision in accounting statements. The report of Deloitte Plender Griffiths and Co. and Price Waterhouse and Co. on the results stated

> 'You will appreciate that the appraisal of stock, contracts and a number of other matters involve the exercise of judgement; they are not matters of precision. Broadly speaking, of the total shortfall of £14.5 millions we would attribute roughly £5 millions

2. THE INSTITUTE OF CHARTERED ACCOUNTANTS OF SCOTLAND RESEARCH AND PUBLICATIONS COMMITTEE, 'Balance Sheets of Investment Trust Companies', (1969).

to adverse differences which are matters substantially of fact rather
than judgement and the balance of some £9.5 millions to adjustments
which remain matters substantially of judgement?[3]

The comment in the Guardian was

'The major point here is that the majority of the AEI losses are
accepted by both sides to be the result of different accounting
processes, and as far as shareholders are concerned they mean little
more really than a paper adjustment.'[4]

The estimation of profit depends to a large extent on consistent
methods of valuation of assets and it is clear that the change in
directors brought about a reappraisal of the methods adopted in the
past, and led to a more conservative value of stocks and contracts.
As profit is only a fraction of the assets employed in most companies
a change in asset values has a disproportionate effect on the profit
of that year—if a company earns 15% on its assets a 5% difference
in asset values make a 33% difference in the profit. In the case of a
company with large contracts on which progress payments have been
received the amount estimated for work in progress is much larger
than the net amount shown on the balance sheet because of the
deduction of progress payments. In the case of AEI it was stated that
a 5% difference in the value of stocks, work in progress and
outstanding orders would amount to £15 million.[3]

*6.3 Statements of Standard Accounting Practice*
The second stage in the development of accounting standards began
in 1969 when the Council of the English Institute issued a 'Statement
of Intent on Accounting Standards in the 1970's' which heralded a
change in the direction of more precise regulation of the methods of
presenting accounting statements. In particular the intention was
expressed of advancing standards along the following lines:

'1.    Narrowing the Areas of Difference and Variety in Accounting Practice.
The complexity and diversity of business activities give rise to a
variety of accounting practices justifiably designed for and
acceptable in particular circumstances. While recognising the

3. *Accountancy*, September 1968, pp. 632–4.
4. MCCLACHLAN, SANDY, *The Guardian*, 30 July 1968, p. 10.

impracticability of rigid uniformity, the Council will intensify
its efforts to narrow the areas of difference and variety in
accounting practice by publishing authoritative statements
on best accounting practice which will, wherever possible, be
definitive.

2. Disclosure of Accounting Bases.
The Council intends to recommend that when accounts include
significant items which depend substantially on judgements of
value, or on the estimated outcome of future events or
uncompleted transactions, rather than on ascertained amounts,
the accounting bases adopted in arriving at their amount should
be disclosed.

3. Disclosure of Departures from Established Definitive Accounting
Standards. The Council intends to recommend that departures from
definitive standards should be disclosed in company accounts or in the
notes thereto.

4. Wider Exposure for Major New Proposals on Accounting Standards.
In establishing major new accounting standards the Council will
provide an opportunity for appropriate representative bodies
to express their views by giving wide exposure to its draft proposals.

5. Continuing Programme for Encouraging Improved Accounting Standards
in Legal and Regulatory Measures.
The Council will continue its programme of suggesting appropriate
improvements in accounting standards established by legislation,
of which the proposals on "Companies Legislation in the 1970's"
submitted to the President of the Board of Trade in March this year
are an example. The Council will also continue to support and
encourage the improvement of accounting standards in relevant
regulatory measures such as the City Code on Take-overs and Mergers
and Stock Exchange requirements.'[5]

The Accounting Standards Steering Committee was formed in
association with the Scottish and Irish Institutes and was later joined
by the Institute of Cost and Management Accountants and the
Association of Certified Accountants; the Committee also drew upon
a number of other bodies representing industry and finance. The
Committee has embarked upon an extensive programme dealing with
many different aspects of accounts and has made a practice of issuing
exposure drafts 'to give those concerned with financial reporting,

5. *Accountancy*, January 1970, pp. 2–3.

whether as preparers or users of accounts, the opportunity to express their views'[6] before issuing definitive statements.

Once the standards are formally promulgated it is intended that members of professional bodies responsible for preparing accounts should be obliged to use them, or if significant departure from those standards occurs the effects of such difference should be clearly disclosed and explained. The obligation extends to the auditors; in the words of the English Institute:

> 'All significant departures from accounting standards made by the directors in preparing the accounts should be referred to in the auditors' report, whether or not they are disclosed in the notes to the accounts.'[7]

In other words the intention is that, when standard practices have been defined, one will be able to assume that the accounts are drawn up on that basis unless the auditor draws attention to the variation in his report. It is worth noting, however, that unless there is a change in company law incorporating the new standards the sanction is limited to the disciplinary powers of the professional bodies over their members. In the words of the foreword to the Statements, issued by the English Institute:

> 'The Council, through its Professional Standards Committee, may inquire into apparent failures by members of the Institute to observe accounting standards or to disclose departures therefrom.'[8]

The provision relating to the disclosure of departure from standards is not however intended to deal merely with companies which refuse to accept them. It is specifically stated that the standards are not intended to be a rigid code of rules; the possibility of creating

6. ACCOUNTING STANDARDS STEERING COMMITTEE, 'Accounting for the Results of Associated Companies', (Exposure Draft), (1970).
7. INSTITUTE OF CHARTERED ACCOUNTANTS IN ENGLAND AND WALES, 'The Effect of Statements of Standard Accounting Practice on Auditors' Reports', U17 (1971) para. 2.
8. INSTITUTE OF CHARTERED ACCOUNTANTS IN ENGLAND AND WALES, 'Explanatory Foreword to Statements of Standard Accounting Practice', para 3.

a code which would deal with all circumstances and developments
is denied, and the chance that a method other than that prescribed
in a standard may be necessary in some circumstances is accepted.
At the same time the need for continuous review of standards in the
light of changes in business practice and the economic environment
is stressed. A set of standards is not, like the laws of the Medes and
Persians unchangeable, but methods are expected to evolve and change
in the light of new needs and developments.

Up to the time of writing three Statements of Standard
Accounting Practice have been issued:

1.    *'Accounting for the Results of Associated Companies'* defines the
      standard practice to be followed by companies or groups of
      companies with investment in associated companies (defined in
      Chapter 4.5). The broad effect is to incorporate in the consolidated
      profit and loss account the share of profits, less losses, of the
      associated companies attributable to the investing company.
      The profits are to be shown both before and after tax and any
      extra-ordinary items of profit or loss are to be disclosed
      separately. The consolidated balance sheet is to show the
      investment in associated companies at cost plus the share of
      profits attributable to the investing company but retained in the
      associated companies (unless the investment is shown at a
      valuation). The investing company's own accounts are not
      affected unless no consolidated accounts are prepared, when
      they will be modified to indicate the information about associated
      companies. Briefly the effect of adopting the standard practice
      is to reveal the total profit earned by the company including
      the earnings of its subsidiaries and the group's share of the
      earnings of associated companies and to indicate the profits
      retained in associated companies as an increase in the book
      value of the investment.

2.    *'Disclosure of Accounting Policies'* requires:

(i)   Explanation if accounts are prepared on the basis of assumptions
      other than those defined as fundamental accounting concepts.
      The fundamental concepts were explained in Chapter 1.6.

(ii)  Disclosure of accounting policies for dealing with items which

are material in determining profit and stating the position
of the company. Because of the variety of accounting methods
which are possible, the knowledge of the policies which are
being followed by the directors is essential to the understanding
of the accounts. This standard practice is therefore an important
one which applies to all companies.

3.    *'Earnings per share.'* This statement, which only applies to
companies having a stock exchange quotation for equity shares
is unusual in dealing with a statistic derived from the accounts,
rather than the accounts themselves. The explanatory note states

> 'A fundamental requirement of financial reporting is the
> disclosure of the salient features of the accounts in the
> clearest possible form. Outstanding among the matters of interest
> to shareholders in quoted companies are earnings per share,
> dividends per share and the trend of these two figures over
> a number of years.'[9]

The statement defines earnings per share as

> 'the profit in pence attributable to each equity share, based
> on the consolidated profit of the period after tax and after
> deducting minority interests and preference dividends, but before
> taking into account extra-ordinary items, divided by the number
> of equity shares in issue and ranking for dividend in respect of
> the period.'[9]

Quoted companies are required to state earnings per share on the
face of the profit and loss account, and it may also be necessary
to state fully diluted earnings per share. The calculation is
discussed more fully in Chapter 8.

Exposure drafts have been issued dealing with:

Accounting for Acquisition and Mergers.
Stocks and Work in Progress.
Accounting for Extra-ordinary Items.

9. INSTITUTE OF CHARTERED ACCOUNTANTS IN ENGLAND AND WALES,
   'Statement of Standard Accounting Practice', M2, (1971).

Accounting for Changes in the Purchasing Power of Money.
The Accounting Treatment of Grants, under the Industry Act 1972.

and other subjects under review include:

The Treatment of Research and Development, Goodwill,
Depreciation, Corporation Tax and Deferred Taxation.
Fundamental Principles of Periodic Financial Statements and Group
Accounts.
Accounting for Diversified Operations.
Accounting for Leases. Treatment of Major Changes in the
Sterling Parity of Overseas Currencies.
Sources and Applications of Funds Statements.
Changes in Accounting Policies. Events occurring after the Balance
Sheet Date.

The exploratory work on accounting for inflation has already been
mentioned in Chapter 3.

The establishment of standards is by no means an easy task.
The draft on extra-ordinary items which is at present being considered
is the second on the subject, because the comments made as a result
of the first draft suggested that fundamental changes were necessary.
There have been fierce debates for several years in the United States
over the use of the 'pooling of interests' or merger method of
consolidating accounts and there is no reason to suspect that it will
be any easier to resolve the problems in Britain. In dealing with stock
valuation there arises not only the problem of whether one method
is suitable for all businesses—in fact the draft recognises that long term
contract work in progress needs separate treatment—but the considerable
effect on both published profits and on taxation of profits which a
change in method could bring about. The Steering Committee have
recognised this and have had discussions with the Inland Revenue in
an attempt to clarify the tax implications, but it is obvious that there
will be strong opposition to any change which might increase the
tax liability of many companies.

The programme of the Committee has been criticised on the
grounds that they are attempting to lay down standards without
first laying down a firm basis of theory, and it is evident from the
standards and exposure drafts already issued that there is some

justification for this criticism. If the basis of accounts is historic cost, then a manufacturing company can find sound reasons for using either a full cost or a marginal cost method of valuing stock. The decision to make it obligatory to use either one or the other is therefore an arbitrary one, the sole justification for which is that it provides comparability through uniformity. Similarly the choice of depreciation method which is expected to be the subject of a draft, must be an arbitrary one. On the other hand, the clear evidence of confusion and disillusionment in the minds of non-accountants, caused by the proliferation of methods has been used to support the need to bring some order into the situation as quickly as possible, without waiting for the results of theoretical studies which are taking place. Perhaps the key to the situation is the acknowledgement that the standards now being established are subject to change. They represent the best which can be achieved in the light of present knowledge and provided a continual review and willingness to change is maintained, the debate created by the exposure drafts and standards will prove useful.

### 6.4 The Stock Exchange

Since 1929 the London Stock Exchange has investigated all new applications for quotation of securities and its powers to deny access to the market enables it to demand publication of more information than is required by the Companies Acts. The Listing Agreement Companies (formerly the General Undertaking), which must be entered into by companies applying for a quotation, includes a number of clauses dealing with financial information, and these tend to be in advance of company law. For example, the Stock Exchange imposed an undertaking to publish consolidated accounts a decade before the law made it an obligation for all companies with subsidiaries, in 1947.

The main obligations as to financial information, contained in the current form of Agreement, may be summarised as follows:

1. To notify the Stock Exchange, without delay, of important information such as dividend and profit announcements, proposed new issues of shares, acquisitions, changes in directors or of any information necessary to enable the shareholders to make proper appraisal of the company.

2.   To circularise to holders of securities, or advertise, a half yearly
     or interim report. The minimum contents of the report comprise
     information on profits, taxation and dividends, but in practice
     there is considerable variation in the amount of detail given.[10]
3.   To include certain information in the annual directors' report.

Some of the listed information is required by the Companies Acts in
any case, but there are some additional requirements, in particular,

(a)   a geographical analysis of trading operations if a company
      or group trades outside the United Kingdom.
(b)   a statement of the country of operation of each subsidiary
      company.
(c)   if the company or group holds 20% or more of the equity
      capital in another company there must be stated the principal
      country of operation of that company, particulars of its share
      and loan capital and reserves and the percentage of each class
      of capital in which the company or group is interested.
(d)   a statement of persons having an interest in a substantial part
      of the share capital of the company. 10% of the nominal value
      of any class of capital having full voting rights is considered
      to be a substantial interest.
(e)   a statement as to whether or not the company is a close
      company as defined in the Corporation Taxes Act 1970.
      The definition of a close company is complicated, but broadly
      speaking it implies control by not more than five persons having
      a share or interest in the capital or income of the company.
(f)   if the auditors have stated that the accounts are not drawn up
      in accordance with the standard accounting practices approved
      by the accountancy bodies a statement of the reasons for adopting
      an alternative basis.
      The influence of the Stock Exchange is not confined to the
Listing Agreement. In 1964 the Chairman of the Council of the
London Stock Exchange requested companies to publish in the

10. HOLMES, GEOFFREY, reviewed 'Interim Statements' in *Accountancy* September
    1971, pp. 518–22.

annual report a ten year summary of the main financial figures. This request has not been incorporated in the Listing Agreement but a large number of companies do provide a summary, although the contents and the length of time covered vary considerably. Out of 300 companies reviewed in the Survey of Published Accounts 1970–71, 72 companies published summaries covering less than 10 years, 162 summarised figures for 10 years or more and 66 did not publish any summary. Profits and losses were the only items contained in all the summaries. The next most popular items were dividends (222) and capital employed (213). One of the least popular elements of the summary was the flow of funds statement (9 companies) although 66 companies published current funds statements.[11] Other information which the Stock Exchange recommends companies to provide includes the date of purchase of major fixed assets shown in the balance sheet at cost, rents payable for land and buildings, and the method used in calculating depreciation.

*6.5 Summary*

Professional accountants and the Stock Exchange have both had a big influence on the quality of financial information published by companies. The most significant activity at the present time is the work of the Accounting Standards Steering Committee which is reviewing many aspects of published accounts with the intention of setting sound standards, which must be observed in practice and which will eliminate unnecessary variety in methods of reporting. The Statements of Standard Accounting Practice issued by the Committee are already causing major changes in published accounts and one should expect further changes as new standards are created.

11. INSTITUTE OF CHARTERED ACCOUNTANTS IN ENGLAND AND WALES, 'Survey of Published Accounts 1970–71', pp. 145–6.

# 7 Company Law

'. . . *it is difficult to imagine any single piece of information potentially more misleading than that which forms the foundation of the present accounts, namely the annual profit figure* . . . .'[1]

*7.1 Development of Company Law*

Although the Companies Act 1907 required a statement in the form of a balance sheet to be included in the annual return, sent by each company to the Registrar of Companies, it was not until 1929 that the law prescribed any of the contents of the accounts. The Companies Act 1929, required directors to produce a balance sheet and profit and loss account in every calendar year and lay them before the company in general meeting and to send copies to those entitled to notice of general meetings. The Act specified a limited amount of information to be contained in the balance sheet, but with the exception of the need to disclose directors' fees the contents of the profit and loss account were not prescribed. Since that time the Companies Acts 1948 and 1967 have made considerable changes and the 2nd schedule to the 1967 Act, which contains most of the accounting provisions, extends to more than 14 pages.

Many companies have been prepared to provide more information than the law required and it could be written in 1940:

1. ROSE, HAROLD, 'Disclosure in Company Accounts', Eaton Paper No. 1, Institute of Economic Affairs, 1965, p. 19.

'What effect the revised Companies Act of 1929 had on the general form and shape of the company accounts it is difficult to assess . . . in general, however, private endeavour was moving so far ahead of the new Companies Act that it was, so to speak, left standing.'[2]

In 1945 the Cohen Committee reported:

'The amount of information disclosed in the accounts of companies varies widely. The recent tendency has been to give more information and this tendency has been fortified by the valuable recommendations published from time to time by the responsible accounting bodies as to the form in which accounts should be drawn up and the information which they should contain. The directors of many, but by no means all, companies now give shareholders as much information as they consider practicable and the accounts which they present contain much more detail than is required by law.'[3]

One major development in response to changing methods of company operations was the production of consolidated accounts. As has already been shown in Chapter 4, if a company operates through subsidiary companies, the holding company accounts may disclose very little and may even be extremely misleading. The Dunlop Rubber Co. Ltd appears to have been the first company to produce a full consolidation, which it did for the year 1933,[4] although there was much opposition to the concept and it was not until 1948 that consolidated accounts were made compulsory.[5] There were provisions in the 1929 Act requiring companies to give information about subsidiaries but these were largely nullified by the proviso

'that it shall not be necessary to specify . . . the actual amount of the profits or losses of any subsidiary company, or the actual amount of

2. The Editor of 'Finance and Commerce' in 'The Accountant', 'Among the Balance Sheets'. Gee and Co. 1940, pp. 1–2.
3. Report of the Committee on Company Law Amendment, 1945, H.M.S.O. Cmnd 6659, para 97.
4. The Dunlop Accounts are discussed by the Editor of 'Finance and Commerce' in 'The Accountant', 'Among the Balance Sheets', Gee and Co. 1940, pp. 7–16.
5. KITCHEN, J, The Accounts of British Holding Company Groups, *Accounting and Business Research*, No. 6, Spring 1972, provides a full account of the attitudes to disclosure in the early years.

any part of any such profits or losses which has been dealt with in any particular manner.'[6]

A similar development in the 1960's was the practice, of some companies, of bringing into their accounts their share of the profits and losses of companies which were not subsidiaries but in which they had a substantial interest. This method of dealing with Associated Companies has been confirmed by the Statement of Standard Accounting Practice referred to in Chapter 6.3 but has not yet been made compulsory by law.

### 7.2 Profits and Dividends

One purpose of published accounts is to show whether the company has sufficient profit to cover the dividends paid to the shareholders. The need to calculate distributable profit arises from the rule that dividends are not to be paid out of capital, which implies that there must be a balance of profit at least equal to the distribution to be made. Both directors and auditors may be liable for dividends paid out of capital through their negligence.

The definition of distributable profit is vague and has to be deduced from the decisions of the Courts in a number of cases. In the words of the Jenkins Report:

'The method by which the profits of a company are to be ascertained depends on circumstances which may vary widely as between one company and another. The only general rule that can with any certainty be deduced from the decisions of the Courts in the cases in which this matter has been considered is that profits must be ascertained by reference to normal standards of commercial prudence.'[7]

Profit is normally brought into account when it is realised and as a general rule realised profits calculated in accordance with accepted accounting principles are distributable. In calculating trading or revenue profits the realisable value of any current assets remaining at

6. The Companies Act 1929, section 126 (1).
7. Report of the Company Law Committee 1962. H.M.S.O. Cmnd 1749, para 335.

the end of the period must be at least equal to the balance sheet
value, but market values of fixed assets are not necessarily taken into
account. Thus whilst provision is made for doubtful debts and for the
reduction of the realisable value of stock below cost, fixed assets may
remain at cost or at cost less a conventional deduction for depreciation.
There is some doubt as to whether depreciation is a necessary charge
in calculating profit and the Jenkins Report recommended that this
should be made obligatory.[8] Realised capital profits such as those
arising from the sale of fixed assets also appear to be distributable,
without reference to the values of other fixed assets remaining with the
company. The Jenkins Report considered that such profits should only
be distributable

> 'if the directors are satisfied that the net aggregate value of the
> assets remaining after the proposed distribution of that profit,
> will be not less than the book value, so that the share capital
> and reserves, remaining after the distribution, will be fully
> represented by the remaining assets.'[8]

Because the basis of the restraint on distribution is in the rule
against paying dividends out of capital, it is possible to ignore past
losses and pay dividends out of subsequent profits. Once capital has
been lost, it is not possible to pay it out as dividend or in any other
way. The Jenkins Committee accepted this in respect of capital losses,
but considered that the revenue account should be a continuous account
so that past revenue losses should be made good before current profits
are distributed.[8]

If a company revalues assets the question of whether it is
permissible to distribute surpluses from such revaluation may be raised.
The law as it stands is confused because in one case[9] it was decided
that it was not and in another case[10] it was decided that it was.
The Jenkins Committee recommended that the law should make it

---

8. Report of the Company Law Committee 1962. H.M.S.O. Cmnd 1749,
   para 350.
9. Westburn Sugar Refineries Ltd vs Inland Revenue Commissioners 1960,
   S.L.T. 297.
10. Dimbula Valley (Ceylon) Tea Co. Ltd vs Laurie (1961), ch. 353.

clear that unrealised capital surpluses should not be available for dividend.[8]

The recommendations of the Jenkins Committee referred to above have not been incorporated in legislation and the law remains vague on this subject. In most cases this does not matter, because accounts are drawn up on a conservative basis and most companies have substantial retained profits which are unlikely to be distributed, because the funds they represent have been invested in the business.

A special problem arises when a company holds shares in another company and that other company pays a dividend out of profits earned before the date of acquisition by the company which holds the shares. The conservative accounting treatment would be to recognize that the dividend represented a distribution of assets paid for when the shares were bought and deduct the amount from the cost of the asset in the balance sheet. There is no clear rule of law, however, which would prevent the company from taking the dividend into the profit for the year and using it to pay a dividend to its own shareholders. If the shares had been paid for by the issue of shares in the acquiring company this course of action would not necessarily leave the assets overstated in the balance sheet, because the cost of the investment may have been recorded as the nominal value of the shares issued in payment. It is not satisfactory that a company should be able to buy profits and possibly give a misleading impression of its earning power for a period of time and the Jenkins Report recommended that with limited exceptions companies should be prohibited from distributing such amounts. This question has been discussed more fully in Chapter 4.4.

### 7.3 Secret Reserves

Up to about 1940, the main purposes of published accounts appear to have been to show whether the company was solvent and whether there was sufficient profit, including undistributed profits of previous years, to cover the dividend. It was accepted that the balance sheet was a historical document, that assets should be stated at cost or below cost, and that it was permissible to err on the side of understating assets but not to overstate assets. This was summed up by one critic in the following words:

'In England it seems to be well established that a public accountant is not a valuer and that a balance sheet prepared and certified by him may misrepresent the facts to any extent, provided they confine this misrepresentation to understatement.[11]

This view of the accounts led to the creation of secret or undisclosed reserves by excessive writing down of assets or overstating liabilities and adjusting profits accordingly. For example Paton and Baldwins Ltd which was engaged in the wool textile trade maintained a stock reserve (deducted from the amount of stock in the balance sheet and not disclosed separately) to counteract the effect of fluctuations in wool prices. The chairman gave some information at the annual general meeting in 1936, in connection with a new issue of capital which was to be made, and disclosed that whilst the previous five years' profits shown in the accounts totalled £1,688,223 actual profits were £2,033,223. The profits in this period had been smoothed as well as reduced in total, in that four years had been reduced by a total of £420,000 and one year increased by £75,000.[12]

In similar vein the chairman of Tube Investments Ltd is reported as saying:

'We bring in only just as much (profit) as we require to pay the dividends we recommend, and to place to general reserve, or add to the carry forward, so much as we consider will make a pretty balance sheet.'[13]

These are not exceptions but part of the general pattern. It is obvious that investors might be seriously misled by the existence of such reserves, especially if used to smooth the profits of a company, and the seeds for change were sown by the Royal Mail Case.[14] The Royal Mail Steam Packet Co. had for several years made substantial reserves for taxation in excess of the current liability for tax,

11. MACNEAL, K, Truth in Accounting, Pennsylvania U.P., 1939, p. 24.
12. The Editor of 'Finance and Commerce' in 'The Accountant', 'Among the Balance Sheets', Gee and Co., 1940, p. 81.
13. The Editor of 'Finance and Commerce', in 'The Accountant', 'Among the Balance Sheets', Gee and Co., 1940, p. 59.
14. Rex vs Kylsant (1932), 48, T.L.R. 62.

thus reducing profits and showing a conservative balance sheet.
The details of the tax charge and liability were not disclosed so that
shareholders were unaware of the extent of the reserves. During the
years 1921–26 the reserve was reduced by transfers to profit and loss
account, thus increasing the profits of those years without disclosing
that this had been done. Whilst the balance sheet was still on a conservative basis, the profitability was overstated. Except for 1926,
the transfers were on a fairly small scale and the auditor accepted
them as reasonable, but in 1926 a loss of £300,000 was converted into
a profit of £439,000 which he felt should not be approved without
drawing attention to it. The net profit was therefore described as
'including adjustment of taxation reserves', although the amount of
the adjustment was not stated. Both the chairman and the auditor
were charged with criminal offences in connection with the issue of
accounts knowing them to be false but were acquitted, although
the chairman Lord Kylsant was found guilty on a similar charge
connected with a prospectus for an issue of debentures. Evidence was
given by leaders of the accounting profession that the method of drawing
attention to the change in reserves was accepted practice.

Despite the obvious deficiency of accounts containing such
undisclosed reserves, it was not until 1948 that their creation was
prohibited, although there appears to have been some modification
in practice in the years following the Royal Mail Case.

*7.4 Current Legislation*
Major amendments of the Law were made by the Companies Act 1947,
which was consolidated with the 1929 Act in the Companies Act 1948.
The amendments were the result of the Cohen Report published in
1945 in which it was stated

> 'The present legal requirements as to the contents of accounts to be
> presented to shareholders are too meagre. The practice of showing
> a number of diverse items in one lump sum and thereby obscuring
> the real position as to the assets and liabilities, and as to the
> results of trading, makes it difficult and often impossible for a
> shareholder to form a true view of the financial position and
> earnings of the company in which he is interested.'[15]

15. Report of the Committee on Company Law Amendment 1945, H.M.S.O.
Cmnd 6659, para 7(d).

The remedy which was suggested by the Cohen Committee
and adopted by the 1947 Act was to provide that the balance sheet
shall give a true and fair view of the state of affairs of the company,
that the profit and loss account shall give a true and fair indication
of the earnings or income of the period, to prescribe in considerable
detail what must be disclosed in the accounts including the separate
statement of reserves, and to require companies with subsidiaries to
prepare consolidated accounts in addition to the holding company's
balance sheet, except in a limited number of cases. Secret reserves
were not to be allowed except in the case of banking companies,
discount companies and assurance companies where special
considerations of the need for stability and public confidence over-ruled
the shareholders' right to information. Whilst outside the scope of their
enquiry, the Cohen Committee drew attention to the importance of
informed Press comment and suggested that the law of libel might
be considered to see if freedom of comment could be reasonably
encouraged.

The trend towards greater disclosure was continued in the report
of the Jenkins Committee in 1962 many of the recommendations of
which were incorporated in the Companies Act 1967. The Jenkins
Committee report endorsed the importance of disclosure of as much
information as was reasonably required but also pointed to the limits
of the process. One must consider:

> 'whether the additional information would be of any real value to
> the person receiving it, and if so whether its ascertainment would
> involve an amount of work disproportionate to its value, or its
> publication might be detrimental to the company's business, and
> thus indirectly to its shareholders and creditors.'[16]

*7.5 The Over-riding Requirement—A True and Fair View*
The accounting provisions contained in the Companies Acts 1948
and 1967 may be summarised as follows. In addition to its obligation
to send copies of the accounts to members and debenture holders every
company is required to file annually with the Registrar of Companies

16. Report of the Company Law Committee 1962, H.M.S.O. Cmnd 1749,
    para 13.

a copy of its audited balance sheet and profit and loss account, together
with copies of the auditors' and directors' reports.[17] The accounts are
therefore open to inspection by anyone. There is an over-riding
requirement that the balance sheet shall give a true and fair view of
the state of affairs of the company as at the end of its financial year
and that the profit and loss account shall give a true and fair view of
the profit of the company for the financial year, supported by specific
rules as to the information to be disclosed, most of which are contained
in the 2nd Schedule of the Companies Act 1967. The force of the
over-riding provision was emphasised by the Jenkins Committee (who
were of course commenting on the Companies Act 1948 and in
particular the accounts provisions of the 8th Schedule of that Act).

> '. . . we doubt if it is always appreciated that the accounts which
> comply with the requirements of the Eighth Schedule. . . . may still
> fail to give the true and fair view required by the Act, although we
> think this is the effect of section 149 (3) which requires that the
> duty to give the detailed information required by the Eighth
> Schedule is without prejudice to the general duty to give a
> true and fair view.'[18]

Nevertheless, the 'true and fair view' is to be interpreted in
the technical sense of complying with good accounting practice.
The Acts say little about the basis to be adopted but it was made
plain by both the Cohen and Jenkins Committees that they accepted
the historic basis of the accounting statements and both rejected the
idea that the balance sheet should reflect the value of the company.
The Jenkins Report quoted with approval and at length a passage
from the Recommendations on Accounting Principles issued by the
Institute of Chartered Accountants in England and Wales 'because we
think that the function of company accounts may not be fully
appreciated by those investors unfamiliar with accounting principles
and practice.' Part of the quotation is as follows

> 'The primary purpose of the annual accounts of a business
> is to present information to the proprietors, showing how their

17. Before 1967 the class of exempt private companies had the privilege of
    not filing accounts but this is now discontinued.
18. Report of the Company Law Committee 1962, H.M.S.O. Cmnd 1749,
    para 332.

funds have been utilised and the profits derived from such use. It
has long been accepted in accounting practice that a balance
sheet prepared for this purpose is an historical record and not a
statement of current worth. Stated briefly its function is to
show in monetary terms the capital, reserves and liabilities of
a business at the date as at which it is prepared and the manner
in which the total moneys representing them have been
distributed over the several types of assets. Similarly a profit
and loss account is an historical record. It shows as the profit
or loss the difference between the revenue for the period covered
by the account and the expenditure chargeable in that period,
including charges for the amortisation of capital expenditure. Revenue
and expenditure are brought into the account at their recorded
monetary amounts. This basis of accounting is frequently
described as the historical cost basis. . . .'

The Report goes on

'In our view this "historic cost" basis of accounting, which
was endorsed by the Cohen Committee and is used almost
universally, should continue to be the basis on which company
accounts are prepared.'[19]

However as the Jenkins Report points out 'the law does not
and should not insist upon a rigid and uniform application of the
historical cost principle in all circumstances.'[20] Valuation of assets
is permitted and supplementary information may be necessary to give
a true and fair view. The law does not and cannot prescribe in detail
what is true and fair in all circumstances and it is left to the judgement
of the directors and the auditors to decide by reference to normal
commercial standards. One would expect therefore a continuation of
the process of change in accounting statements that has taken place
in the past, as accountants attempt to adapt to new circumstances and
to improve the quality of the information.

19. Report of the Company Law Committee 1962, H.M.S.O. Cmnd 1749,
    para 333.
20. Report of the Company Law Committee 1962, H.M.S.O. Cmnd 1749,
    para 334.

*7.6 Minimum Contents of Published Accounts*
A long list of items which must be disclosed, forms the main body of
the accounting provisions in the Companies Acts. Most, but not all,
of the provisions are gathered together in the 2nd Schedule to the
Companies Act 1967 but they tend to be mixed up and without any
real order. A full summary of the statutory requirements has therefore
been given in the Appendix (page 169). In order to indicate the scope
of the information which will be contained in published accounts a
brief summary, including explanations is given here. The contents of
the accounts are as follows:

1.  The *balance sheet* is to summarise the share capital, liabilities
    and assets, with such particulars as are necessary to disclose
    the general nature of the assets and liabilities.
2.  *Reserves, provisions, liabilities* and *assets* are to be classified under
    headings appropriate to the company's business. Fixed assets,
    current assets and assets that are neither fixed nor current are
    to be separately identified. The term provision is defined by the
    Act as:

    > 'any amount written off or retained by way of providing
    > for depreciation, renewals or diminution in value of
    > assets or retained by way of providing for any known liability
    > of which the amount cannot be determined with substantial
    > accuracy.'[21]

In general, amounts written off an asset will be deducted from
that asset in the balance sheet; liabilities will be classified with
other liabilities. A provision should be distinguished from a
reserve. The creation of a provision reduces profit and therefore
reduces reserves, which represent part of the equity shareholders
interest in the company. The use of the terms 'retained' and
'set aside' is a little misleading in that there is no specific
appropriation of assets involved in the making of a provision
—merely the charging of expense to profit and loss account and
the creation of the liability or writing down of the asset.

21. Companies Act 1967, Sch. 2, para 27.

The creation of the separate category of assets which are
neither fixed nor current owes its introduction to the Jenkins
Report which suggested that in some cases it might be misleading
to classify an asset under one or other heading, for example, a
balance due to a holding company on current account or a debt
owing for goods sold on extended credit. In practice there is a
fair amount of flexibility in the grouping of assets and liabilities
in the balance sheet.

3.   *Financial structure*—a considerable amount of detailed information
is required to give a clear picture of the capital and liabilities
of the company. This includes dates and terms of redemption
of redeemable preference shares and repayment of loans,
options on unissued shares, charges on assets, movements on
reserves and provisions, and contingent liabilities.

4.   *Methods of calculation.* The methods of arriving at the amount
of fixed assets is required to be stated. In most cases this will
comprise a statement of cost, aggregate depreciation written
off since the assets were acquired and the remaining book value.
If an asset has been revalued then the value and aggregate
depreciation since the valuation will be stated and the date of
valuation must also be given. Some exceptions are made, notably
goodwill patents and trade marks, and investments in subsidiary
companies for which it is sufficient to show the book value at
the balance sheet date. If investments are brought into the
balance sheet at market value at the balance sheet date there
is no need to disclose the cost. The manner in which the amount
attributed to work in progress and stock in trade is computed
is also to be stated. The requirement of the Act is not sufficient
to produce precise statements of the basis of stock valuation
and most companies seem content with a general statement
such as 'lower of cost and net realisable value'.

5.   *Current Values.* A statement of current market values is required
in the case of

(i)   Quoted investments held by the company. If the market value
is higher than the stock exchange value then the stock exchange
value must also be shown. In the case of unquoted investments
in equity share capital the directors may estimate the value.

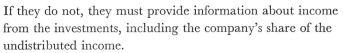

If they do not, they must provide information about income from the investments, including the company's share of the undistributed income.

(ii) Interests in land (including buildings on the land). The directors report must indicate the difference between the book value and the market value of the interests if it is significant to members or debenture holders.

6. *Miscellaneous.* The Act specifies in detail a large number of classifications which must be shown separately, including such items as loans to employees to buy shares in the company, loans to officers of the company (including repayments during the year), certain expenditures carried forward as assets such as preliminary expenses and costs of issue of shares and debentures.

7. *The Profit and Loss Account.* The prescribed contents of this account are a miscellaneous collection of revenue and expense items. Under revenue the company must disclose turnover (if it exceeds £250,000), rents of land and income from investments. Turnover is not defined but the Jenkins Committee suggested that an appropriate description would be

> 'the total amount receivable by a company in the ordinary course of its business for goods sold or supplied by it as a principal and for services provided by it.'[22]

A number of expenses must be disclosed including depreciation, loan interest, hire of plant and machinery, remuneration of auditors and emoluments of the chairman, the directors, and employees receiving more than £10,000 p.a. The directors' report is also to state the average number of persons employed by the company or the group in the United Kingdom and aggregate remuneration paid in respect of the year covered by the accounts, unless the number is less than 100.

Details must be given of the charge for taxation and dividends, both paid and proposed, for the period of the account.

22. Report of the Company Law Committee 1962, H.M.S.O. Cmnd 1749, para 394.

If the profit and loss account is affected by unusual transactions or by a change in the basis of accounting details must be disclosed.

8.  *Comparative Figures.* In both the balance sheet and the profit and loss account the corresponding amounts of the previous year are to be shown. The Jenkins Report suggested a summary of certain key figures for the previous 5 years should be required but although this was not put into the Act, many companies do provide summaries of both balance sheet and profit figures for periods of from 5 to 10 years.

9.  *Group Accounts.* A holding company is obliged, unless it is a wholly owned subsidiary of another company incorporated in Great Britain, to produce group accounts. These will normally be in the form of consolidated accounts.

10. *Other information* must be given in the accounts or in the directors' report. The information is varied in nature and ranges from the principle activities of the company, through analysis of turnover and contribution to profit of different classes of business, to details of political and charitable contributions if they exceed an aggregate amount of £50.

11. There are *exemptions from disclosure of information*, particularly information about reserves, in the case of banking, discount, insurance and shipping companies. The effect of the exemptions is to allow secret reserves in such cases. The clearing banks have ceased to take advantage of the exemptions.

*7.7 Summary*

Attitudes to published accounts have changed a great deal over the last 40 years. In the 1930's it was still meritorious to understate profitability; secret reserves were regarded as necessary to maintain a strong financial position; the only sin was to be optimistic in stating the net assets of the company.

Changing opinions as to what companies should publish were given legislative force by the Companies Act 1948 which called for full disclosure and outlawed secret reserves. The traditional historic cost basis of accounts was not seriously disturbed but the emphasis was placed on providing a true and fair view. The 1967 Act continued the process of requiring more to be disclosed and also compelled all companies to make their accounts available to the public through the Registrar of Companies. Before 1967 a large number of family companies, termed exempt private companies, were entitled to restrict publication to members and debenture holders. At present, the published balance sheet contains a vast amount of detail but the profit and loss account is still a very abbreviated statement disclosing very little of the expense structure of the company.

# 8 Interpretation of Accounts

*'Accountants and financial analysts are reluctant to admit the fact,*
*but company accounts are normally very difficult to interpret.'*[1]

## 8.1 Introduction

The published accounts provide a valuable source of information
about a company but they contain a mass of data and one needs to
conduct a methodical examination in order to distinguish what is
important from that which can be passed over. The first thing to
remind ourselves is that the accounts are historical statements with a
limited purpose—'to present information to the proprietors, showing
how their funds have been utilized and the profits derived from such
use.'[2] They provide a collection of statistics about past transactions
of the company, including a statement of the obligations and assets
arising out of those transactions, but no attempt is made to value
the company. As historical documents their primary purpose must be
that of control—to indicate whether the company is performing in
accordance with expectations and if not, to draw attention to aspects
which are out of line. Their use is primarily to provoke questions
rather than to provide answers, although in practice they are
inevitably used in forming expectations about the future.

1. Points from Published Accounts, *Accountancy*, February 1969, p. 118.
2. INSTITUTE OF CHARTERED ACCOUNTANTS IN ENGLAND AND WALES.
   'Recommendations on Accounting Principles', N15, para 1.

Secondly, although some figures will be more important than others, it is not reasonable to expect the whole of the operations of the company to be summed up in one or two reported figures such as profit or total assets. On the contrary, much of the detail which is important for understanding what is taking place may be relegated to notes, in order to present a clear overall profile in the main statements, and a careful reading of the whole of the accounts is necessary.

Thirdly, the accounts must be read in context and other sources of information must not be overlooked. The annual report contains the auditors' and directors' reports which should be read as part of the accounts. If the accounts have not been drawn up in accordance with accepted practice in any material particular one would expect the auditor to draw attention to this in his report.[3] The directors' report contains accounting data such as the analysis of turnover and profit between different classes of business, market value of interests in land and buildings, and remuneration of employees, as well as other relevant information about the company. The chairman's statement is often issued with the annual report and may give useful information about the past year and about events subsequent to the date of the balance sheet and expectations for the future. A full analysis of a company will not cease after the perusal of the annual report. An appraisal of the success or otherwise of a company needs a standard with which to compare the results achieved and this leads to the examination of the accounts of other companies in the same trade. Results achieved by a company will often be strongly influenced by the general economic situation and the state of trade in the industry. Identification of such relationships will be important in any attempt to forecast future profitability. Although our discussion must be restricted to the examination of the accounts, real understanding requires a great deal of other information.[4]

3. The auditor does not report on statements other than the accounts. In particular he takes no responsibility for the directors' report or supplementary statistical data in the annual report.
4. A full account of the analysis of business conditions may be found in MORRELL, JAMES, 'Business Forecasting for Finance and Industry', Gower Press,

The use of the accounts will differ according to the interest of the reader. A creditor is mainly interested in whether the amount owing to him is likely to be paid on the due date. He is primarily interested in the liquidity and solvency of the company. A shareholder is also concerned that the company can pay creditors on the due date, because of the detrimental effects of default, but he is also concerned to obtain some indication of profitability and growth. It is convenient, therefore, to discuss the accounts from the wider viewpoint of the shareholder, in the knowledge that in so doing we will cover a number of points of interest to creditors. One point is worth emphasizing in this connection. For the shareholder the consolidated accounts of the group are usually the most informative; they are drawn up to provide the members of the company (the shareholders) with full information about the group. In the words of the auditors' report, the consolidated accounts are designed to give a true and fair view 'so far as concerns members of the company'. For creditors and minority shareholders in a group the relevant accounts are those of the company against which they have claims. The consolidated accounts will be misleading in that the separate legal existence of the different companies in the group is ignored.

Even from the shareholders' point of view the overall summary provided by the consolidated accounts is obtained by sacrificing a great deal of information which might be obtained by having, say, the accounts of the major subsidiaries. There is a cost attached to reducing the statements to manageable size. Usually the best outside standard for assessing performance is that provided by a comparison of the results of other firms in the same industry. If a group has diverse interests in several industries which are merged in the consolidation the degree of comparability is reduced. Even comparison with previous years of the same company may be difficult if much change in the composition of the group occurs.

The use of accounting data has generally depended on experience, judgement and intuition, which makes it difficult to do more than draw attention to some aspects of the accounts which are regarded as being significant. For example, in discussing the process of bond rating in the United States, J O Horrigan comments:

'Moody's, in particular, rejects the idea that its rating system can be reduced to a quantitative formula. It stresses that it gives great weight to non-statistical factors—that is, non-quantifiable factors —and its chief rater, Mr. Edmund Vogelius, is quoted as saying "It is a judgement of analysts. No computer can come up with a rating".[5]

Even so, it is possible to identify some methods which have proved useful in sorting out the data and forming an opinion and we are acquiring a growing body of experimental work which will be referred to briefly in the course of the discussion. In general the method of using the accounts consists of identifying a number of figures, which may be absolute amounts taken directly from the accounts or more frequently ratios calculated from the statements, and comparing them with a standard. The standard is derived from previous accounts of the same firm or from the accounts of other companies. Our discussion will begin with a consideration of the use of trends in the company's own accounts and then continue with a more general discussion of some significant ratios.

### 8.2 Trends

A single set of accounts taken in isolation is not likely to be very informative, and the first step in the analysis will be to set out the results of several years side by side. The published accounts give the previous year's figures but it is desirable to have displayed at least five years results. Many companies set out the main figures for five or ten years in a statistical section of the annual report. The purpose of this step is to draw attention to changes which have taken place and to identify trends, regular changes such as may be due to a trade cycle, and irregular fluctuations which may denote instability and therefore greater risk. In addition to the absolute figures taken directly from the accounts it will be useful to calculate a number of ratios and compare them over the same period. For example the growth of profit over time may be due to increased efficiency in the use of resources, to the investment of additional capital or a combination of the two. The use of the ratio of profit/capital employed takes

5. HORRIGAN, J O, 'The Determination of Long Term Credit Standing', *Journal of Accounting Research*, Empirical Research in Accounting 1966, p. 48.

account of capital changes and so provides an indicator of changes in efficiency. Such ratios may provide insight into the financial structure of the company and contribute to the forecasting of the future position. They also provide a convenient means of making comparisons between companies in that differences in size are eliminated by the calculation. We therefore have two standards which can be used in appraising a company—its own past history and the results of other companies trading in similar circumstances. Financial ratios provide a convenient means of making both comparisons.

Because we expect some stability in the affairs of a company the perusal of the accounts is expected to give some guidance as to the future. Unless there is a major change of policy one would expect the financial structure to change slowly; if very rapid change takes place because of mergers and acquisitions then the value of the accounts in forecasting will be much reduced. There is no support, however, for the simple projection of trends of profit. There are too many different influences on profit for this to be a valid exercise. Richard A Brealey describes one test, which was made, of the usefulness of past profits in forecasting future profits. Four companies were selected at random and an index of earnings for the period 1950–57 was compiled for each. Five investment analysts were asked to rank the companies in order of expected earnings for 1957–58 using only the information about past earnings. Note that the analysts were not asked to forecast the amount of earnings, but merely to state which company would produce the highest earnings, the next highest and so on. The experiment continued by selecting another four companies and five analysts and so on until 48 companies had been reviewed by 60 analysts. The results achieved were similar to those which might have been achieved by ranking the companies at random; there was no evidence that the trends of profit were of any assistance in forecasting the next year's result.[6] This does not mean that one should not trust analysts or that accounting data are worthless. It is a warning against naïve projection of past trends without consideration of other influences.

6. BREALEY, RICHARD A, An Introduction to Risk and Return from Common Stocks, M.I.T. Press, 1969, Ch. 8.

As a counter to this example, the persistence of profitability, measured by pre-tax return on net assets,[7] *relative to the average profitability of the industry* has been shown to provide a useful guide to future results. Even so it is stressed that this is an average result which is of more use in picking a portfolio of companies than in forecasting the results of a single company.

'. . . we are predicting averages rather than individual events. . . we can hope to provide rules for predicting the average future profitability of a group of companies, but we cannot hope to make accurate predictions about a single individual company. We can . . . provide a simple rule which will select from a group of companies a subset which will have higher average future profitability than the group as a whole, but this subset may contain some individual companies whose profitability will be worse than the average of the whole group, as well as some which will have exceptionally high profitability.'[8]

*8.3 Earnings per Share*

For examining trends, earnings per share (EPS) is a number which has a great deal of significance for the shareholder. It is of sufficient importance to have been the subject of the third Statement of Standard Accounting Practice, issued by the Accounting Standards Steering Committee,[9] which stated that EPS should be shown on the face of the profit and loss account and the basis of calculation should also be shown. Earnings are the normal source of dividends and the trend of earnings may be expected to be correlated with the trend of dividends. If a company issues new shares, however, whether for cash or in acquiring other companies the trend of earnings is not sufficient guide to the old shareholders. It is possible for the existing shareholders to suffer a decrease in earnings at the same time as the total earnings of the company are increasing. EPS indicates the position of the existing shareholder after allowing for the new capital.

7. This is described in chapter 9, ratio 7a, return on investment.
8. WHITTINGTON, GEOFFREY, 'The Prediction of Profitability,' Cambridge, 1971, page 232.
9 See chapter 6.3.

The concept is a simple one, the ratio being defined as

$$\frac{Earnings}{Number\ of\ equity\ shares\ issued\ and\ ranking\ for\ dividend}$$

where earnings is defined as the profit after tax and after deducting minority interests and preference dividends. If a substantial amount of new capital is issued part way through a year a weighted average number of shares should be used to take into account the fact that the company had the use of new capital for only part of the period. The use of the ratio to indicate trends over time makes it imperative that the comparative figures for previous periods be calculated on the same basis. In particular:

(a)     If new equity shares have been issued as fully paid, out of reserves (a bonus issue) the company receives no new capital but merely transfers from reserves to share capital a sum equal to the nominal amount of shares issued—it capitalises reserves. Because the total capital, consisting of share capital plus reserves, has not changed, the ratios of previous years must be recalculated on the basis of the number of shares existing after the bonus issue. For example, a company having steady earnings of £20,000 per annum and 50,000 shares has earnings per share of 40p. If it then issues another 50,000 shares by capitalising reserves the current EPS falls to 20p, although there is no real change in the position of the shareholders. The calculation for previous years must be restated in terms of the current share capital if valid comparison is to be made. Because the old shares comprise one-half of the revised capital the old EPS must be halved to 20p per share.

(b)     A new issue of shares may be offered to existing shareholders at a price below the existing market price (a rights issue). In such a case there is a bonus element, but also an addition to the resources of the company. The adjustment recommended by the Statement of Standard Accounting Practice is based on a separation of the bonus element in the issue. In the above example assume that instead of a bonus issue the company had issued 50,000 shares at £1 per share, the market price of the old shares before the rights issue being £2 per share. The theoretical market price of the shares after the rights issue may be calculated as follows:

| | | |
|---|---|---|
| Market value before the issue | 50,000 at £2 | £100,000 |
| New issue of shares | 50,000 at £1 | £ 50,000 |
| Total market value of 100,000 shares | | £150,000 |

which gives a share value after the rights issue of £1.50 per share. If the company earns the same rate of return on the additional £50,000 capital which it has received as it earned on the market value of its shares before the issue earnings will increase by 50% to £30,000 and EPS will be 30p in the future. The same result could have been achieved by issuing 25,000 shares at the market value of £2 per share and then issuing 25,000 bonus shares. Thus the bonus element represents a quarter of the total share capital, and adjustment of the comparative figures may be made by multiplying the old EPS by three-quarters (which is equivalent to increasing the ' number of old shares in the denominator by the proportion of bonus shares issued). The revised EPS for previous years is 30p.

As the figure of EPS is likely to be regarded as an indicator of future EPS, account should be taken of any factors which are known to exist and to affect the future. If a company has issued equity shares which do not rank for dividend until a later date, or loan stock which is convertible into equity shares, the current EPS is likely to be a misleading guide to the future. This has led to the recommendation that in addition to the current EPS there should be calculated the 'fully diluted EPS' on the basis that all the equity ranks for dividend and the conversion of the loan stock has taken place. Similarly if options or warrants to subscribe for shares have been granted (for example under an executive incentive scheme) the fully diluted EPS should take account of the effect of the subsequent issue of the shares. If new shares are subscribed for, additional capital will be received by the company and earnings must be increased by the expected earnings on such capital. The basis recommended by the Statement of Standard Accounting Practice is to assume that the return on the additional capital will be equivalent to that on an investment in $2\frac{1}{2}\%$ Consolidated Stock.

There are no perfect indicators and EPS is no exception. A rising trend of EPS is desirable but may be misleading in the short term. Assume Company A and Company B have each issued 100,000 shares. A has EPS of 30p and B has EPS of 60p but the market value of a share in either company is the same because whilst B's earnings are stable A's earnings are growing rapidly. If the companies were to merge to form a new company with a combined share issue of 200,000 then EPS would be 45p. From the point of view of shareholders in A this appears to represent growth whereas all that has happened is that they have exchanged part of the expected growth in the future for immediate profit. Similarly B's shareholders have exchanged immediate profit for part of A's future growth. Assuming that the market price before the merger accurately reflected the values of the shares then it is possible for A to pay too high a price for the merger and still appear to have gained. Thus if B's shareholders were issued with 150,000 shares in A, to give a total capital of 250,000 then the EPS would fall to 36p, which appears to be a gain to A but in fact involves a substantial capital loss. This illustrates the short term nature of the accounting statements, something which can only be overcome by forecasting future trends.

*8.4 EPS and Taxation*

From 1 April 1973 the change in the taxation of profits and dividends will make the EPS a more ambiguous indicator. Up to that date earnings represents the maximum amount made available for dividend by the current year's operations and the relationship between earnings and dividend indicates the cover for the dividend. Exceptions to this are companies with overseas profits bearing low rates of tax on which additional tax would have to be paid on remittance to the United Kingdom. After 1 April 1973 part of the corporation tax on profits will be imputed to, or regarded as payment of tax on, the dividend. The effect will be that whilst earnings which have borne United Kingdom tax will still represent the maximum amount made available for dividend, the dividend will be measured net, after deducting personal tax at the standard rate instead of gross, before tax. At the proposed rates of tax this will mean that the amount available for gross dividend will be 10/7 of the earnings. There will therefore be a break in the trend of EPS in 1973. On the other hand if earnings are wholly from overseas, and foreign tax is such that no UK corporation tax is payable, the interpretation of EPS will be similar to that applying up to April 1973 because there is no UK tax to impute to dividends. An example is as follows:

| *Up to 1973* | Profit | | | 1,000 |
|---|---|---|---|---|
| | Corporation Tax (40%) | | | 400 |
| | Earnings | | | 600 |
| | Maximum dividend from current | | | |
| | earnings (gross) | | | 600 |

| *From 1973* | Profit | | | 1,000 |
|---|---|---|---|---|
| | Corporation Tax (50%) | | | 500 |
| | Earnings | | | 500 |
| | Maximum dividend from current | | | |
| | earnings | Gross | 714 | |
| | | Less tax | 214 | 500 |

The comparable figures for dividend are 600 and 714. If the whole of the earnings consisted of profit bearing tax overseas at the rate of 50% then the maximum dividend would be 500 gross of which 150 would be remitted to the tax authorities and 350 to the shareholders (subject to any transitional relief).

It has been suggested that in order to make the EPS a consistent indicator the definition of earnings should be amended to the maximum dividend which could be paid from current profits—in the illustration this would be 714 in the case of the UK profits and 500 in the case of overseas profits. This definition has the added advantage that EPS/Dividend per share reflects the cover for the dividend. On the other hand the practical difficulties of estimating hypothetical taxes on overseas profits will probably prevent its adoption.[10]

The treatment of deferred taxation is important in interpreting earnings and any ratio derived from earnings, and the rate of tax on profits as well as any notes on taxation should be checked. In so far as earnings are used as an indicator of growth or of cover for dividend, an abnormally low tax charge due to accelerated depreciation may give a misleading picture. If the company makes provision for deferred tax, the amount charged in the profit and loss account will be a normal rate but such a provision is not obligatory and some companies merely charge the current liability to tax in the profit and loss account.

## 8.5 Price Earnings Ratio

A common use of earnings per share, which is not easy to explain, is in the price earnings ratio, which is the relationship between price per share and earnings per share. In theory, price is related to the expected flow of dividends (including distributions of capital) and to the extent that dividends are related to earnings there must be a relationship between earnings and price. If a constant dividend is expected in perpetuity then the dividend yield (dividend per share/price per share) is the true rate of return on the investment made at that price. If continual growth in the dividend is expected at rate $g$ then it can be shown that the true rate of return from the investment is equal to the dividend yield plus the rate of growth.[11] If the proportion of earnings distributed is expected to remain constant so that $D = aE$

10. See ACCOUNTING STANDARDS STEERING COMMITTEE, 'Notes on Accounting for Corporation Tax under the Imputation System', 1972, paras. 24 and 25.

11. Let $D$ = expected dividend at the end of the year.

$g$ = expected rate of growth in dividend.

$k$ = rate of return required by the investor      $k > g$

$$\text{Price } (P) = D \left( \frac{1}{1+k} + \frac{1+g}{(1+k)^2} + \frac{(1+g)^2}{(1+k^3)} + \ldots \right) = \frac{D}{k-g},$$

$$\therefore \frac{D}{P} = k - g \quad \text{or} \quad k = \frac{D}{P} + g.$$

(where $D =$ dividend and $E =$ earnings) then the true rate of
return $(k)$ is equal to $aE/p$ plus growth or $(a/PE$ ratio$) + g$.
Alternatively $PE$ ratio $= a/(k - g)$. The $PE$ ratio is therefore dependent
on the proportion of earnings distributed $(a)$, the rate of return on
investment expected by shareholders $(k)$, and the rate of growth $(g)$.
If we assume that a company distributes $2/3$ of its earnings at present,
that shareholders require $10\%$ on capital (before deducting personal
tax) and that growth of dividends will continue at the rate of $5\%$ per
annum after the first five years the following combinations may occur
amongst many others:

| | | | |
|---|---|---|---|
| Dividend yield at the present time | $5\%$ | $4\%$ | $2\frac{1}{2}\%$ |
| Expected annual growth of dividend | | | |
| for the first five years | $5\%$ | $10\%$ | $20\%$ |
| Price/Earnings ratio | 14 | 17 | 26 |

Each of the combinations represents the same $10\%$ return on the
investment in the shares. There is no simple relationship between
$PE$ ratio and return, and the only way to determine it is to make
explicit the assumptions about growth and to evaluate the stream of
dividends which is expected.

*8.6 Some Empirical Work*
Because the use of accounts is mainly based on intuition and
judgement there is little direct evidence of the value of any particular
accounting data. In recent years a number of attempts have been
made to test the usefulness of ratios for particular purposes and before
discussing specific accounting ratios in more detail it is relevant to
mention some of the empirical work which has been done in this
field. The discussion is intended to illustrate rather than to be a full
review of the subject. It will be sufficient for our purpose to deal
briefly with three reports from the United States, two of which are
concerned with solvency and one with performance. If we are to
provide anything other than an assertion that such and such ratios are
generally recommended by the experts, we must have some evidence
linking patterns of ratios with company results. One test of the
usefulness of ratios is their ability to predict—can ratios be identified

which are good predictors of future events? Is it possible to predict
that a company will fail to pay its creditors before it actually defaults?
Can we select companies which are likely to grow rapidly?

W. H. Beaver[12] attempted a direct test of accounting data by
comparing ratios of a sample of 79 firms which had defaulted with
a paired sample of firms which had not defaulted. Default (or to use
Beaver's term, failure) was defined as the inability to pay financial
obligations as they mature. In fact 59 firms were declared bankrupt,
16 failed to pay a preferred stock dividend and 4 represented other
failure. One half of the sample, selected at random was used to
determine the value of a selected ratio which best divided the
sub-sample into failed and non-failed firms—that is, if most of the
failed firms had a lower ratio, most of the other firms had a higher
ratio and vice versa. The choice of the critical value was made by
ranking the firms in order according to that ratio and judging
which value would produce the smallest number of wrong
classifications. The ratio was then used to classify firms in the other
sub-sample into predicted defaulters and non-defaulters, and the result
compared with actual experience.

A cursory glance at average ratios of defaulting firms
compared with average ratios of other firms might suggest that it
should be easy to classify firms using one or more ratios. For example
the average ratio of total debt to total assets[13] for Beaver's sample
of firms which failed was 51%, five years before failure and rose to
79% one year before failure. The same ratio for the average
non-defaulting firm was less than 37% throughout the period. The
possibility of discriminating individual companies is reduced,
however, by the considerable range of ratios which occurs in both
categories—from less than 10 to 160% for failed and from less than
10 to 80% for non-failed companies. Even one year before failure 16%
of companies which defaulted had total debt less than 40% of total
assets.

Nevertheless the results of Beaver's test suggested that even
using a single ratio, predictions could be made up to 5 years before

12. BEAVER, W H, Financial ratios as Predictors of Failure, *Journal of
    Accounting Research, Empirical Research in Accounting*, 1966, pp. 71–127.
13. The ratios mentioned here are discussed in chapter 9.

the event which were substantially better than could be reasonably attributed to chance. Moreover the tests identified the longer term ratios such as net income/total assets and total debt/total assets as better predictors of default than those involving current assets and liabilities. It was also significant that there was considerable deterioration in the ratios of defaulters over the five-year period which was studied. In a later paper[14] Beaver suggested that default tends to be determined by permanent factors—if the basic position is sound and profit prospects are good a company will recover from a temporary shortage of liquid assets, but if the long term position is unsound then even a good liquid position will not prevent winding up. One problem of attempting to assess the usefulness of the information by its ability to predict the outcome is that the outcome may be altered because of the warning given to management by the data. This will apply especially to the current position where a trend in the wrong direction will tend to be brought to the notice of management fairly quickly and pressures will develop to correct the situation. Whilst the study supports the use of long term ratios therefore it does not mean that the current position can be ignored. Persistence of a poor liquid position over time, and particularly persistent deterioration, will sound a warning.

Although the usefulness of single ratios is of interest, the analyst is better able to draw conclusions from the combined effects of several pieces of data. J. O. Horrigan[15] used a number of ratios in combination, and studied their relationship with potential default by a company. The bond ratings of Moody's and of Standard and Poor have been demonstrated to be good indicators of risk of default and Horrigan's test was based on the ability of the ratios to predict the bond rating. Although the actual systems adopted by the rating agencies take into account a much wider field of information, the results of Horrigan's test were good and suggested that accounting data can play a significant part in the detection of risk of default.

14. BEAVER, W H, Alternative Accounting Measure as Predictors of Failure, *Accounting Review*, January 1968, pp. 113–22.
15. HORRIGAN, J O, The Determination of Long-Term Credit Standing with Financial Ratios, *Journal of Accounting Research, Empirical Research in Accounting*, 1966, pp. 44–70.

The combination of data selected as providing the best prediction included ratios measuring long term solvency (equity/debt), short term capital turnover (working capital/sales), long term capital turnover (sales/equity) and profit margin (net operating profit/sales), together with the figure of total assets and a variable indicating the legal status of the bond.

A third study deals with the prediction of performance rather than solvency, performance being measured in terms of rise in price of the shares over a period of time. R. E. Jensen[16] used the technique of cluster analysis to attempt to identify natural classifications in a sample of 113 shares traded on the New York Stock Exchange. Using measurements of a number of characteristics the process of cluster analysis compares each pair in a sample to find the two which are most alike, which then form a group of two. The process is repeated with the group already formed treated as a single unit having the average characteristics of the group. At each repetition either new pairs are formed or groups join together until at the final stage all merge into a single group. The interest lies in the intermediate groups which are formed and whether the classifications at any stage appear significant. In Jensen's study the cluster analysis was made on data for the period 1949–53 and the result compared with the subsequent performance of the companies in the period 1954–65. Those companies which performed well, in terms of percentage gain in price in the later period tended to remain as isolated units in the cluster analysis of the earlier period. In other words those companies were sufficiently different from other companies to prevent their joining a cluster until late in the programme, and the differences in the characteristics were sustained for a period sufficiently long to make their identification worthwhile. The 9 characteristics used by Jensen were sales trend and variability, earnings per share and dividend per share, debt/equity ratio and four market indicators.

*8.7 Summary*

Analysis of accounts is largely dependent upon the ability to select relevant information from the mass of data which is published, appraise

16. JENSEN, R E, A Cluster Analysis Study of Financial Performance of Selected Business Firms, *Accounting Review*, January 1971, pp. 36–56.

it by reference to experience drawn from the history of the company or other companies and convert it into an expectation for the future. Such analysis must draw upon knowledge of the general economic situation, the outlook for the industry in which the company operates and of other companies, as well as the information contained in the reports and accounts issued by the company. There is a great variety of information which may be obtained from the accounts including such diverse aspects as the size of the company, the composition of its assets and the way it is financed, the need for new finance for capital expenditure commitments and loan repayments and the trend and variability of profits. In a limited discussion one must select, and and the next chapter will concentrate on a number of financial ratios which are commonly used to assess the solvency and profitability of a company. The ratios used are generally based on personal judgement of what is relevant, but there has been some empirical work involving the use of ratios and some of this work has been briefly described.

*Suggestions for Further Reading*

HELFERT, E. A., Techniques of Financial Analysis, Irwin.

FOULKE, R. A., Practical Financial Statement Analysis, McGraw-Hill.

# 9 Ratio Analysis

*'If one could rely on accurate information, navigation would be a simple science, whereas the art and great fascination of it lies in deducing correctly from uncertain clues.'*[1]

## 9.1 Introduction

The aim of this chapter is to discuss a number of ratios which can make a contribution to the analysis of the financial position and results of a company. The ratios must be dealt with one at a time although their real significance will usually depend on the way they combine. What is important is the way the company functions as a whole and in the longer term. A current shortage of cash will probably be overcome if the underlying trading position is good, whilst surplus cash may be dissipated quickly if substantial losses are incurred by ill-considered ventures. The trend of a ratio, indicating improvement or deterioration will usually be more significant than the absolute amount at one point in time.

Two groups of ratios make a significant contribution to an orderly analysis of the financial affairs of a company, those dealing with solvency or ability of the company to pay its creditors both in the short and in the long term, and those dealing with profitability or efficiency of operations. The groups are by no means mutually exclusive, if only for the reason that there is often a pay-off between

1. CHICHESTER, FRANCIS, 'The Lonely Sea and the Sky',

solvency and profitability. A company may be able to ensure solvency by holding sufficient cash, but only at the cost of unremunerative use of that asset. It will be much more secure if it uses equity finance rather than borrowing on fixed terms, but may pay more for its capital. Nevertheless the broad classification is a useful one.

*9.2 The Current Position*

Of the solvency ratios there are two balance sheet ratios dealing with the short term liquid position

1. The *current ratio*, defined as

$$\frac{Current\ assets}{Current\ liabilities}.$$

As a rule of thumb for the average manufacturing company an optimum ratio of 2/1 is often quoted, but wide variations from this figure can be observed. For example in the sample of ratios given in Table 9.1 there are 20 companies in mechanical engineering. The average (median) ratio was 2.07 but one-quarter of the ratios were below 1.80 and one-quarter above 2.35. A relatively high ratio denotes greater asset backing for the liabilities, and therefore less risk of inability to pay, but may indicate inefficiency in holding an abnormally high proportion of unremunerative current assets. Other ratios will throw light on this aspect. The current ratio includes in the numerator the stock in trade which may not be readily realisable, except at much reduced prices, and preference is often given to a second liquidity ratio, which ignores stock.

2. The *quick ratio* (or 'acid test'), defined as

$$\frac{Liquid\ assets}{Current\ liabilities}$$

where liquid assets are defined as current assets, other than stock and work in progress. The quick ratio compares the cash in hand and amounts receivable from debtors and short term investments with the liabilities payable in the near future. The rule of thumb for this ratio is 1/1 but again this is a very broad indicator and many companies appear to function quite well with a smaller ratio.

Table 9.1 *Liquidity Ratios*

| Industry | No. of companies | Current ratio | | | Quick ratio | | |
|---|---|---|---|---|---|---|---|
| | | LQ | M | UQ | LQ | M | UQ |
| Mechanical engineering | 20 | 1.80 | 2.07 | 2.35 | 0.78 | 1.00 | 1.28 |
| Manufacture of wool and worsted and rags and blankets | 17 | 1.72 | 2.18 | 3.18 | 0.56 | 0.97 | 1.18 |
| Builders merchants | 14 | 1.62 | 1.80 | 1.85 | 0.78 | 1.05 | 1.31 |
| Department and general stores | 18 | 1.53 | 1.85 | 2.20 | 0.65 | 0.99 | 1.26 |

*Source:* Dun and Bradstreet. Business Ratios.[2] LQ = Lower quartile. M = median. UQ = Upper Quartile.

2. Dun and Bradstreet. Business Ratios. Winter 1968. Table 5, p. 44.

In using any ratios involving current assets and liabilities it is important to remember that they may fluctuate considerably in the normal course of trade, especially in a seasonal trade, and that it is possible to improve the ratios by 'window dressing'. Consider a company with the following working capital at two different dates:

|                   | June  | December |
|-------------------|-------|----------|
| Stock in trade    | 2,000 | 1,000    |
| Cash and debtors  | 2,000 | 2,000    |
|                   | 4,000 | 3,000    |
| Less creditors    | 2,000 | 1,000    |
|                   | 2,000 | 2,000    |

A reduction in purchases in December has caused the reduction in stock and creditors and has increased the current ratio from 2/1 to 3/1 and the quick ratio from 1/1 to 2/1. The ratios need to be judged in the light of any seasonal influences of this sort. If a company draws up accounts at a time when stock holding is relatively small it will tend to appear abnormally liquid. Window dressing takes place when action such as the running down of stocks is taken with the sole purpose of creating a favourable picture.

*9.3 The Long Term Position*
In the longer term, the solvency of the company may be judged by two ratios, one from the balance sheet and one from the profit and loss account.

3. The *gearing* (or leverage) *ratio* defined as Debt/Equity where debt consists of the long term borrowing of the company and equity is equity share capital and reserves.[3] An alternative measure of gearing is Debt/(Equity and Debt) which measures the proportion of long term capital provided by long term liabilities. As a rough guide

3. The discussion of gearing has been based on figures drawn from the accounts and the measurement is affected by the asset values adopted by the company. An alternative measure may be based on market values.

it has been suggested that most manufacturing firms would find it
costly to raise further long term debt if the debt/equity ratio after
the new issue significantly exceeded 1/2.[4] In other words it is
acceptable for a company to borrow one-third of its long term capital
needs on terms requiring payment of a fixed rate of interest. A
selection of average debt/equity ratios calculated from the Summary
of Industrial Profits and Assets published by *The Economist*[5] is given
in Table 9.2.

*Table 9.2 Average Gearing Ratios*

| Industry | No. of Companies | Debt/equity ratio (%) | Times Interest covered | Liabilities* cash flow |
|---|---|---|---|---|
| Building materials | 24 | 24.9 | 12.9 | 2.0 |
| Engineering | 66 | 30.6 | 10.1 | 3.1 |
| Misc. Manufacturing | 69 | 31.0 | 20.8 | 3.0 |
| Breweries, Distilleries & Wines | 13 | 42.2 | 7.2 | 2.7 |
| Catering & Entertainment | 14 | 61.0 | 12.5 | 2.9 |
| Food Manufacturing | 15 | 45.1 | 10.4 | 3.9 |
| Shops, Stores & Distributors | 17 | 20.6 | 15.9 | 3.2 |
| Oil | 2 | 2.6 | 311 | — |
| Property | 45 | 93.7 | 1.8 | 258 |

Based on *The Economist*. Industrial Profits and Assets, July–Sept. 1969.
Debt = Long term loans, preference capital and minority interests.
Equity = Ordinary capital, reserves and deferred taxation.
*See ratio 6 in text.

The average ratios conceal a wide range of gearing and this
is illustrated in Table 9.3 based on an analysis of 2117 British companies
by Prusmann and Murphy.[6] With gearing measured, in this case, by
reference to debt/(equity + debt), 419 firms (19.8%) had gearing of

4. MERRETT, A J and SYKES, ALLEN, 'The Finance and Analysis of Capital
   Projects', Longmans, 1963, p. 113.
5. *The Economist*, Industrial Profits and Assets, July–September 1969.
6. PRUSMANN, DAVID and MURPHY, GEORGE, Gearing in British Quoted
   Companies. Business Ratios. Dun and Bradstreet, Winter 1968, pp. 18–25.

less than 10% whilst 237 firms (11.2%) had gearing of more than
50%. This spread of gearing was found in the analysis by industry
and also by size of firm. The gearing measure in this analysis includes
bank overdrafts as debt with the result that the ratios are slightly
higher than would be found if debt had been restricted to long term
loans.

Financial ratios are not very precisely defined and care is
needed in making comparisons that the measurements are consistent.
Preference share capital has some characteristics of debt and some
of equity and it may be classified with either. Fortunately it forms a
relatively minor source of capital and rarely makes much difference.
Minority interests contain both equity and preference capital.
Deferred taxation is a more general problem. It may be regarded
as a loan from the Government free of interest or as a reserve and
therefore part of the equity. As companies need not show deferred
taxation in the balance sheet perhaps the simplest rule is to treat it as
part of the equity when it occurs. Borrowing from banks is theoretically
short term borrowing, and is included in current liabilities, but in
some cases it may be obvious that there is a hard core of permanent
capital in this category and that some adjustment should be made
for this.

4. The ratio of

$$\frac{\textit{Profit before charging interest and tax}}{\textit{Interest payable}}$$

is a test of the ability to continue to pay charges, imposed by
borrowing on fixed terms, out of variable earnings. It is an alternative
measure of gearing based on the division of income instead of on
balance sheet figures. A minimum 'cover' of 5 times is regarded as
normal for manufacturing companies. The number of times which
interest is covered and the balance sheet measure of gearing of the
company are linked through the rate of return which the company
can earn on the investment of its capital. If interest on loans is payable
at the rate of 10% per annum, a debt/equity ratio of 1/2 and interest
cover of 5 times implies a return on investment of 17% per annum.
On average much higher rates of cover are experienced as illustrated

Table 9.3 Gearing Ratios

| Industry | No. of Companies | Gearing less than: | | | | | |
|---|---|---|---|---|---|---|---|
| | | 10% | 20% | 30% | 40% | 50% | 75% |
| All companies | 2117 | 419 (%) 19.8 | 811 (%) 38.3 | 1234 (%) 58.3 | 1591 (%) 75.2 | 1880 (%) 88.8 | 2104 (%) 99.4 |
| Breweries, Wines Spirits & Drinks | 66 | 3.0 | 19.7 | 47.0 | 71.2 | 89.4 | 100 |
| Chemicals & Plastics | 76 | 27.6 | 55.2 | 75.0 | 84.2 | 97.4 | 100 |
| Drapery and Stores | 179 | 20.2 | 37.0 | 56.5 | 76.0 | 87.2 | 98.9 |
| General Engineering | 269 | 25.3 | 44.4 | 67.7 | 81.1 | 93.7 | 100 |

Source: Prusmann and Murphy.[6]

$$\text{Gearing} = \frac{\text{non-equity funds}}{\text{total fixed capital}}.$$

Non-equity funds = long term liabilities + preference capital and minority interests + bank overdrafts. Total fixed capital = non-equity funds + equity capital and reserves.

in Table 9.2. The figures in that table show the cover for all interest payable including bank and other short term interest.

A widespread problem of comparability of ratios is caused by the basis of valuation adopted in the balance sheet combined with the effects of changing prices. This is accentuated by differing policies of revaluing assets. If fixed assets are revalued, which usually implies an increase in value, equity is increased and the debt/equity ratio is decreased, suggesting a more conservative financial structure. Profits are not affected unless assets which are subject to depreciation are revalued in which case the profits decline and the cover for interest declines. A general agreement to issue statements adjusted for price level changes would go some way to overcome this problem. Another problem affecting comparability is that of leasing of fixed assets. The Jenkins Report recommended that the profit and loss account should show separately rents paid for land and buildings and for plant and machinery and commented

> 'It is becoming increasingly common for companies to sell their freehold properties and take them back on lease from the purchaser and to hire instead of buying machinery and plant. We think the shareholder should be told how much of the company's gross earnings are committed in this way to meet its obligations in respect of rent; these obligations are economically the equivalent of depreciation and interest on debentures and other fixed loans which are already required to be shown separately in the profit and loss account.'[7]

The Companies Act 1967 required companies to show sums payable in respect of the hire of plant and machinery but ignored the recommendation in respect of rent of property. Leasing has been called 'off balance sheet financing', and it is clear that whilst many plant leases are practically equivalent to a purchase of plant with a simultaneous loan repayable in a period shorter than the life of the plant, no reference to either the asset or the indebtedness appears in the balance sheet. The company with a substantial proportion of leased assets will appear to be much lower geared than a similar company which has borrowed to finance the purchase of assets. A

7. Report of the Company Law Committee (1962), H.M.S.O. Cmnd 1749, para 383.

report on the accounts of an American company, J. C. Penney Company Inc.,[8] compared the debt/equity ratio calculated direct from the balance sheet ignoring leases, the ratio calculated using analysts' estimates of the equivalent debt implied by the lease payments reported, and that using the company's own evaluation of the equivalent debt. The debt/equity ratios were as follows:

| | |
|---|---|
| Ignoring leases | 19% |
| Incorporating company's valuation | 62% |
| Using analysts' smallest estimate | 94% |
| Using analysts' largest estimate | 218% |

With such a wide spread of possible estimates the usefulness of the ratio is practically destroyed and there is an urgent need to review the methods of reporting lease obligations.

*9.4 Cash Flow and Solvency*

The financial ratios at any point of time provide a quick check on the position based on experience of what a healthy company looks like. The balance sheet ratios emphasise asset cover for liabilities; they seek to answer the question—in an emergency and allowing for losses arising from forced sale is it possible to pay creditors? One might term it a break up point of view. The ultimate test of the solvency of a company as a going concern is the availability of cash when obligations fall due for payment. For management control, a forecast of cash flows for some period ahead is an essential tool in testing the validity of decisions and financial policies. As published accounts do not normally include forecasts an alternative test, which adopts a going concern point of view, is to calculate how rapidly liabilities could be reduced from the normal cash flow of the company. Cash flow may usually be regarded as the sum of the depreciation and the net profit, after deducting interest and preference dividends. If no new capital expenditure is incurred and no dividend on ordinary shares paid for a time, the cash flow is available to reduce liabilities.

8. AXELSON, KENNETH S, Needed: A Generally Accepted Method for Measuring Lease Commitments, *Financial Executives Magazine*, July 1971.

In examining the short term liquidity of the company in terms of cash flow, we need, first, to define net current liabilities as the difference between current liabilities and liquid assets (debtors, cash and assets immediately convertible into cash). A net current liabilities figure of zero is equivalent to a quick ratio of $1/1$. If the terms of credit given to customers are similar to those received from suppliers, then zero net current liabilities suggest that the cash flowing in from debtors plus cash in hand will be sufficient to pay creditors as they fall due for payment. This is the equilibrium position. If current liabilities exceed liquid assets then a measure of the time needed to restore the position to equilibrium is

$$5. \qquad \frac{\textit{Net current liabilities}}{\textit{Annual cash flow}}$$

A ratio of $1/4$ indicates that it would take 3 months of normal cash flow to accomplish this. As tax on profits is not payable until at least 9 months after the end of the financial year, annual cash flow before deducting tax may be used for the very short term.

The corresponding long term ratio is

$$6. \qquad \frac{\textit{Long term plus net current liabilities}}{\textit{Annual cash flow after tax}}.$$

Examples of this ratio in Table 9.2 range from 2 to 4 years cash flow with the exception of the two oil companies with no net liabilities and the property companies in which the security provided by assets is the main factor. The cash flow ratio appears to have some advantage over the debt/equity ratio in that it is not affected by balance sheet values; it remains the same whether assets are revalued or not. It is also less likely to be affected by leasing of plant assets and so provides a better comparison between companies. One cannot ignore the asset backing but the cash flow ratio provides another insight into the financial situation.

### 9.5 Profitability

The first group of ratios which has been discussed has been concerned with the solvency of the company. A second group of ratios is used to assess the profitability of the company.

7. *Return on capital* provides a means of making a rough comparison of profitability in terms of profit per unit of capital employed either as a trend over time or between companies. Two main methods of calculating the ratio may be identified, the difference between them being attributable to the gearing of the company.

7*a*. Return on investment defined as

$$\frac{Profit\ before\ charging\ interest}{Total\ assets}$$

7*b*. Return on equity capital defined as

$$\frac{Profit\ after\ charging\ interest}{Equity\ capital}$$

The relationship between them is illustrated in Fig. 9.1 in which OE shows the position with no gearing, when return on equity equals return on investment. The line *AB* represents the return on equity arising from any given return on investment when the debt/equity ratio is 1/1 and the rate of interest on debt is 10% per annum.

The effect of gearing is to amplify fluctuations in the profitability of the company; a 20% return on investment in the conditions portrayed in the chart provides 30% return on equity, whilst a zero return on investment reduces return on equity to minus 10%. The break-even point (*X*) at which return on equity equals return on investment is the rate of interest on debt. A change in the gearing causes the line *AB* to revolve on the pivot of point *X*, a high gearing causing the line to be drawn at a steeper angle. A change in the interest rate on debt causes the point *X* to move along OE. Thus, the higher the gearing, the larger will be the amplification of the fluctuations in profitability; the higher the interest on debt the higher will be the break even point.

In order to assess the profitability of operations it is useful to be able to eliminate the effects of gearing by using ratio 7*a* (return on investment). By so doing one obtains a rough comparison of the profit earned per £ of investment in assets irrespective of the source of finance. Whilst this improves the comparability of the figures the

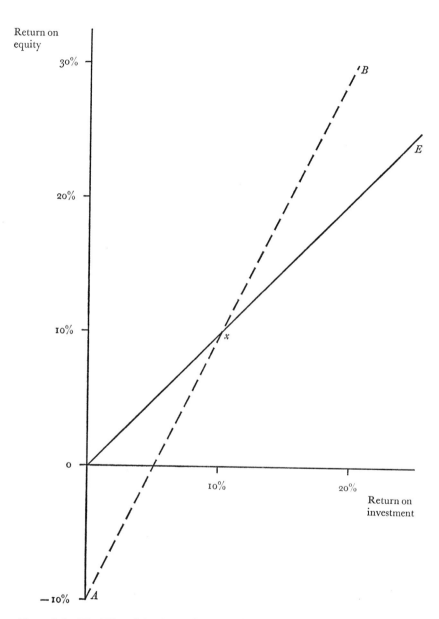

*Figure 9.1   The Effect of Gearing on Return on Equity.*

problems arising from accounting methods which have already been discussed still affect this ratio. To the extent that a company leases assets there is concealed gearing and if this is material some adjustment is necessary. In the case of plant assets an estimate of the cost less depreciation may be added to the total assets, and an estimate of the interest content of the lease payments added to the profit. In the case of land and buildings it may be more convenient to make the opposite adjustment, that is to eliminate the assets from the balance sheet and to reduce the profit by an estimate of the rental value. Because of the differences between companies in the recording of intangible assets such as goodwill it is normal to deduct intangible assets from total assets in calculating return on investment. This improves the comparison in that total assets comprises the sum of the tangible assets for which reasonable consistency between companies may be expected. The uniform use of current asset values in the accounts would further improve the comparability.

*Table 9.4 Return on Investment*

| Industry | No. of companies | LQ (%) | M (%) | UQ (%) |
|---|---|---|---|---|
| Mechanical engineering | 20 | 7.3 | 11.7 | 13.9 |
| Manufacture of wool and worsted and rags and blankets | 17 | 8.0 | 11.0 | 15.7 |
| Builders merchants | 14 | 9.8 | 12.1 | 15.7 |
| Department and general stores | 18 | 10.4 | 16.7 | 21.4 |
| Motor vehicle distributors | 25 | 11.0 | 14.7 | 19.2 |

*Source:* Dun and Bradstreet. Business Ratios.[2] $LQ$ = Lower quartile. $M$ = Median. $UQ$ = Upper quartile. Return on investment is the ratio of profit, before interest and tax, to net assets, defined as fixed assets plus current assets less current liabilities.

Total assets may be interpreted in two ways and care is needed in using ratios to ensure that they have been calculated in the same way. Total assets may be defined as fixed assets plus current assets, or as the sum of fixed and current assets less current liabilities. The latter may be termed net assets. Provided ratios which are being compared are calculated in the same way, there does not appear to be any strong reason for preferring one definition rather than the other.

A sample of ratios is given in Table 9.4 and illustrates the typical wide spread of ratios. In the case of mechanical engineering, for example, one-half the firms had ratios between 7.3 and 13.9% but one-quarter had a return of less than 7.3% and one-quarter a return greater than 13.9%.

*9.6 The Pyramid of Ratios*
It is obvious from a consideration of the steps necessary to calculate return on investment that one is deriving a fairly crude indicator of profitability, which needs to be used in conjunction with other information to build up a picture of what is happening in the company. Although return on investment has been called the 'key ratio' it would be a mistake to treat it as the only evaluator of results. In particular it is unlikely to be a very good guide to the true return on capital which the company earns on its investments. If the company is investing heavily in research the ratio derived from the accounts will be distorted by writing off research expenditure as expense, thus reducing profits, and omitting any asset representing the fruits of research from the balance sheet. In all companies the omission of goodwill from assets causes a difference between the true return on investment and that derived from the accounts. The indicator of profitability provided by return on investment needs to be supplemented by more detailed examination of the figures lying behind the calculation of profit and capital employed.

The study of profitability of a company may be expanded by considering a number of ratios which may be regarded as an analysis of the overall result expressed in the return on investment. The analysis produces a pyramid of ratios, the more important of which are shown in Fig. 9.2. An elaboration of this scheme forms the core of the analysis used in many inter- and intra-firm comparisons.[9] The first stage identifies two main factors contributing to profitability.

8.          $\dfrac{Profit}{Sales}$

9.          $\dfrac{Sales}{Total\ assets}$   or   *asset turnover.*

The product of the two ratios is equal to return on investment. Failure to meet profitability targets may be due to having too much capital tied up in assets which are idle or not fully used, and this weakness will show up in low asset turnover. Alternatively expenses may be too high for the volume of production and sales achieved, and this will be reflected in a low profit to sales ratio. The two ratios are not independent. A reduction in sales will tend to reduce both profit on sales and asset turnover, especially in the short term.

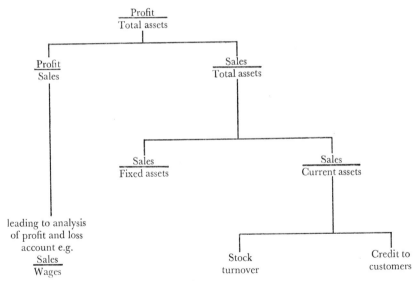

*Figure 9.2    The Analysis of Return on Capital.*

9. A detailed discussion of intra-firm comparison may be found in BRITISH INSTITUTE OF MANAGEMENT, Efficiency Comparisons within Large Organisations. Inter-firm comparison is discussed and illustrated by SIZER, JOHN, in 'An Insight into Management Accounting', Penguin, 1969.

In the case of profit on sales this is due to the existence of fixed costs which do not change with the change in sales. Nevertheless the separation of the two aspects is helpful in identifying weaknesses in the organisation.

Companies in different trades may have very different return on sales and asset turnover ratios, whilst producing similar returns on investment. Fig. 9.3 shows a range of combinations of the two ratios which will produce a return on investment of 15%. For these ratios, therefore, comparison with other companies must be limited to those in the same type of business. A firm in the grocery trade earning

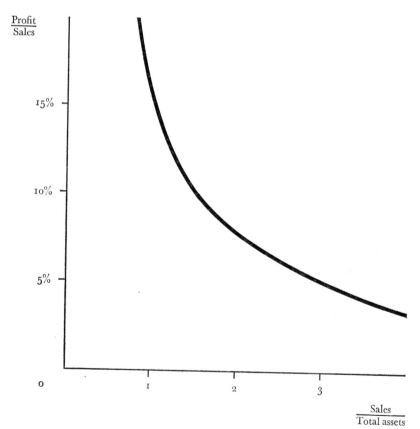

*Figure 9.3    Relationship between Return on Investment,*
*Profit on Sales and Asset Turnover.*

Table 9.5

| | No. of Companies | Profit/sales | | | Sales/net assets | | | Median return on investment (%) |
|---|---|---|---|---|---|---|---|---|
| | | LQ (%) | M (%) | UQ (%) | LQ | M | UQ | |
| Mechanical engineering | 20 | 5.3 | 7.5 | 8.2 | 1.4 | 1.6 | 1.8 | 11.7 |
| Manufacturers of wool and worsted, rags and blankets | 17 | 3.8 | 6.9 | 8.7 | 1.8 | 2.2 | 2.5 | 11.0 |
| Builders merchants | 14 | 2.5 | 4.2 | 5.9 | 2.7 | 3.1 | 4.7 | 12.1 |
| Department and general stores | 18 | 5.9 | 7.5 | 9.3 | 1.6 | 2.0 | 2.5 | 16.7 |
| Motor vehicle distributors | 25 | 2.3 | 3.3 | 4.6 | 3.5 | 4.4 | 5.8 | 14.7 |

Source: Dun and Bradstreet. Business Ratios.[2] LQ = Lower Quartile. M = Median. UQ = Upper Quartile.

1.5% on sales but turning over assets 10 times a year cannot be compared with a machine tool manufacturer earning 10% on sales and turning over assets 1.5 times a year. Some examples of these two ratios are shown in Table 9.5 with the median return on investment for comparison. The median may not be from the same company for each ratio so that the relationship Profit/Net Assets = Profit/Sales times Sales/Net Assets will not be found to exist precisely for these figures.

The ratio of return on sales is analysed by relating expenses to sales, that is by analysis of the profit and loss account. Unfortunately the amount of detail in published accounts is usually too limited to permit a reasonable analysis. One ratio which can be calculated and which throws some light on the efficiency of operations is that involving wages and salaries, often expressed as

9. $$\frac{Sales}{Wages\ and\ salaries}$$

to give a measure of labour productivity. An alternative is to use number of employees in the denominator rather than wages paid, to give a measure of output per head measured by

9a. $$\frac{Sales}{Number\ of\ employees}$$

Information from the balance sheet is sufficient to provide a detailed examination of the asset turnover and in particular the efficiency of management of current assets can be examined by two ratios.

10. $$\frac{Sales}{Stock\ in\ trade}$$

shows the number of times on average that stock is turned over in a year. To be strictly correct one would need to use cost of sales which is not normally published rather than sales, as the stock is valued at cost price. The ratio calculated from the published accounts tends to overstate the rapidity of turnover. The warning about the effects of seasonal changes on the current assets, discussed in connection with ratios 1 and 2, also applies to this ratio. As a general rule a low ratio,

Table 9.6 Current Asset Turnover

| Industry | No. of Companies | Stock turnover (times per year) | | | Debtors collection period (days) | | |
|---|---|---|---|---|---|---|---|
| | | LQ | M | UQ | LQ | M | UQ |
| Mechanical engineering | 20 | 2.9 | 3.3 | 3.8 | 80 | 92 | 98 |
| Manufacturers of wool and worsted and rags and blankets | 17 | 2.7 | 3.4 | 3.8 | 43 | 52 | 59 |
| Builders merchants | 14 | 5.3 | 8.1 | 10.0 | 40 | 70 | 76 |
| Department and general stores | 18 | 7.5 | 8.5 | 9.6 | 28 | 43 | 50 |
| Motor vehicle distributors | 25 | 7.9 | 10.0 | 12.2 | 30 | 39 | 57 |

Source: Dun and Bradstreet. Business Ratios.[2] LQ = Lower Quartile. M = Median. UQ = Upper Quartile.

in comparison to similar companies will indicate poor stock control, possible losses due to obsolescence and spoilage, and illiquidity of the stock. On the other hand a high ratio indicating low stocks may not be a very healthy sign especially if there are other indications of shortage of finance. The trends of the ratios over time will be useful in interpreting the situation.

11.
$$\frac{Debtors}{Sales\ per\ day}$$

provides a measure of the average number of days credit taken by customers, and an indicator of the effectiveness of the credit control exercised by the company. Sales per day is usually defined as sales/365 although other definitions may be used to relate sales to working days. A sample of ratios for current asset turnover is given in Table 9.6.

*9.7 Summary*

In this chapter we have reviewed some of the main ratios which might be used in the analysis of published accounts. Many other ratios can be calculated and the discussion is meant to indicate the method of analysis rather than to be an exhaustive treatment. For example, of the 13 important ratios published by Dun and Bradstreet in the table from which most of the illustrations have been taken, we have not discussed sales/fixed assets, and sales/net current assets although they are shown in the pyramid of ratios. Neither have we considered fixed assets/total assets, stock/net current assets, current liabilities/net worth or net worth/total assets. (Net worth equals the sum of equity capital, preference capital and reserves.) This is not because these ratios are regarded as unimportant. On the contrary each adds a piece to the jig-saw puzzle, the assembly of which produces a picture or profile of the company. But by concentrating on a relatively small number the intention has been to illustrate how the financial structure of the company might be methodically explored, in conjunction with whatever standards might be obtained from other companies or from previous accounts.

In practice one has to select a small number of ratios which will help to illumine the aspect of the company in which one is interested. If the main ratios which have been discussed suggest that one aspect needs special attention it may be useful to examine other ratios reflecting on that aspect. The scheme of analysis in the pyramid of ratios starting with return on investment is a model for the exploration of factors affecting profitability.

# 10 Review and Appraisal

'. . . accounts . . . not to enable individual shareholders to take investment decisions.'[1]

## 10.1 Introduction: The Legal Position

A question which is much discussed is how satisfactory are the accounting statements published by companies. Are there major shortcomings which can be corrected or have we arrived at a situation in which only minor improvement can be envisaged? The answer depends, in part, on what one expects to use the statements for. For what purpose or purposes are they provided? A number of uses of financial information can be identified, some of which are well satisfied by the present type of accounts, but some of which require greatly different information.

The legal position appears to be that the accounts are primarily to direct attention of shareholders to the financial affairs of the company and to provide a basis for collective decisions, such as the declaration of a dividend. Their purpose does not extend to the provision of information for individuals to decide whether to buy or sell shares. Following the case of Hedley Byrne and Co. Ltd and Heller and Partners Ltd (1963) 2 All E.R. 575 the English Institute

1. INSTITUTE OF CHARTERED ACCOUNTANTS IN ENGLAND AND WALES, 'Statement on Accountants' Liability to Third Parties—The Hedley Byrne Decision', 1965, para 8(b).

157

of Chartered Accountants took legal advice on the liability of
accountants to third parties and issued a statement to members
containing the following paragraph:

> *Auditors and shareholders.* In Counsel's view the object of annual
> accounts is to assist shareholders in exercising their control of the
> company by enabling them to judge how its affairs have been
> conducted. Hence a decision by the shareholders collectively taken
> on the basis of negligently prepared accounts and resulting in
> improper payments by or financial loss to the company could
> result in liability. No claim by an individual shareholder, however,
> would succeed in respect of loss suffered through his own investment
> decisions made on the strength of misleading company accounts
> supported by an auditors' report containing negligent
> misrepresentations, since the purpose for which annual accounts
> are normally prepared is not to enable individual shareholders to
> take investment decisions. But if the audited accounts comprised
> in effect part of a document of offer, and the auditors knew or ought
> to have known that the accounts were intended to be so used,
> they could be liable to third parties for financial loss suffered through
> reliance on a negligent auditors' report in connection with
> the offer.'[1]

Despite this, because the accounts are the major source of financial
information, it is inevitable that attempts will be made to use them
as a basis for investment decisions. It is important therefore to
distinguish the uses which are reasonable and the contribution which
the accounts can be expected to make in each circumstance.

### 10.2 Stewardship and the Audit

The primary objective of accounts at the present time may be
described as that of providing means for directors to account for their
stewardship of the funds entrusted to them and in so doing to provide
both an internal check on their honesty and integrity (because they
know they have to account) and the possibility of external check and
criticism. The independent audit of the accounts plays a large part
in verifying that the accounts produced are in accordance with the
records and fairly represent the position. In principle one would
suggest that this purpose of the accounting reports is well satisfied.
Those cases in which failure occurs tend to reflect either weakness in

the audit or the inability of the shareholders to act, rather than any defect in the type of accounting statements which are produced.

One audit problem is created by the existence of groups of companies, each of which is a separate entity and may have a separate auditor. Although relationships between the companies may have a vital effect on the accounts of any one of the group, the auditor may not easily obtain full access to the facts. In the case of the relationship of holding and subsidiary companies the problem is minimal because the control exercised by the holding company should enable the auditors to obtain the information they require—though they still have the problem of deciding to what extent they can rely on the audit performed by others. In the case of associated companies the degree of control is smaller. In the case of companies in which there is no formal relationship but in which the directors of the main company have a substantial interest the possibility of unusual events and situations remaining undetected is at its maximum. An example of the way in which the audit may fail in its purpose is found in the Canadian case of the Atlantic Acceptance Corporation Ltd[2] which defaulted on a $5 million short term note in 1965 and was subsequently found to be insolvent and wound up. Of the total assets of the company, amounting to $150 million, one-third was an investment in the Commodore Group engaged in commercial loan business. These commercial loans were described by the chief executive officer as 'nothing but a can of worms' which in his opinion would have produced about $25 million on a going concern basis, but even this estimate was optimistic. The auditors of the Commodore Group failed to make any comment on the situation, and the auditors of the Atlantic Acceptance Corporation accepted the accounts of that Group without investigation, as they were entitled to do at the time under Canadian standards of practice. In Britain the auditor of a holding company is responsible for reporting on the Group accounts and cannot rely on auditors of subsidiary companies without appropriate enquiry. Nevertheless, the audit problems created by formal or informal relationships between companies are not to be lightly dismissed.

2. FARLINGER, W A, Atlantic Acceptance: Calamity or Catalyst, *Accountancy*, January 1972, pp. 12–16.

It is clearly important that the auditor should be completely
independent of the directors and should be able to resist any pressure
to accept accounts which are doubtful. In theory auditors are appointed
by shareholders to act on their behalf but in practice the directors
will normally take the initiative in choosing the auditors and will
negotiate the fee which is payable by the company. There is no
evidence that this system does not work well in most cases but any
system is likely to break down on occasions and failures do occur.
The enquiry into the failure of Pinnock Finance Co. (Great Britain)
Ltd in 1967 revealed a weakness in the audit without which the situation
of the company would have been disclosed several years earlier and
the losses to investors might have been reduced to relatively small
amounts. Pinnock (G.B.) was used to obtain funds from depositors
in Britain to finance unprofitable companies in the separate Pinnock
Group operating mainly in Australia. The position of the company
depended on the ability of the Group companies to repay loans and
in this sense the basic accounting problem was similar to that in
Atlantic Acceptance. Because appropriate provision for bad debts
was not made, Pinnock (G.B.) accounts showed the position to be
much better than it was. The auditor recognised that the company
was insolvent at the end of 1961 and that the accounts presented to
him for audit did not show the true state of affairs, but because of the
difficulties he experienced in dealing with the directors he decided,
on legal advice, to resign. The report of the Inspectors appointed by
the Department of Trade and Industry stated (without implying any
criticism of the auditors) that if instead of resigning a qualified audit
report had been made 'it is probable that the growth of the company's
activities would have been restricted and in consequence the magnitude
of the eventual failure would have been smaller.'[3] The company
replaced the auditor by an accountant who had previously been
employed by the Pinnock Group in Australia and appears to have
been content to give an unqualified report with a minimum of
investigation, despite being fully informed of the situation by the
previous auditors.

3. DEPARTMENT OF TRADE AND INDUSTRY, 'Pinnock Finance Company
   (Great Britain) Limited and Associated Companies Investigation',
   H.M.S.O., 1971, para 454.

A memorandum of the Scottish and English Institutes of Chartered Accountants at the request of the Department of Trade and Industry[4] suggested, *inter alia*, that future legislation should make it incumbent on a company to report to the shareholders in general meeting the resignation of the auditor before the expiration of his term of office, and that the outgoing auditor should be obliged to state his reason for resigning. Other suggestions have been made for ensuring the independence of the auditor, including the establishment of a panel of judges who would decide all contentious matters in the published accounts, the auditor acting as an advocate with the responsibility of bringing all material facts before the Court. An alternative but smaller step would be to establish an Advisory Board to advise and rule on problems which arise during the course of the audit.[5] With the growth in size and complexity of groups of companies it is likely that new problems will be revealed and there is need for continuous review of the situation. The professional accounting bodies have a big responsibility in this connection.

## 10.3 Solvency

The historical accounts are used as a guide to the ability of a company to pay its creditors and continue operations. Although the tests of solvency are fairly crude they appear to operate well in practice, provided the accounts are reliable and are produced in good time. Although most companies are able to produce accounts within a reasonable time—the Survey of Published Accounts[6] records an average of 120 days and 75% of companies in the survey within 141 days—it is possible for a company to delay its accounts for a considerable period and stronger powers are needed to ensure prompt publication.

The question of obtaining action when the accounts reveal a weak position is another matter. In the case of the Vehicle and General Insurance Co. Ltd, which collapsed in 1971, an analysis of

4. *Accountancy*, March 1972, p. 52.
5. STAMP, EDWARD, The Public Accountant and the Public Interest, *The Journal of Business Finance*, Vol. 1. No. 1.
6. INSTITUTE OF CHARTERED ACCOUNTANTS IN ENGLAND AND WALES, 'Survey of Published Accounts', 1970–71, page 174.

the accounts by the Investors Chronicle as early as 1964 drew attention
to the weak financial position compared with other insurance companies.
Examination of the accounts suggested that the provision for outstanding
liabilities for claims was underestimated and this was subsequently
confirmed by the Tribunal of Enquiry after the collapse.[7] The problem
in this case was not that the accounts failed to provide a warning of
possible financial trouble, for there was clearly anxiety over the
situation in several quarters for a considerable period of time. The
problem was lack of the power and the will to follow up the indicators
which were available, even by experts in the, then, Board of Trade.
The shareholders of most companies are in a weak position. In theory
they hold the ultimate authority in the company and have the power
to dismiss inefficient directors and appoint new ones. In practice it is
difficult for shareholders to take action when there are large numbers
of small shareholdings.

An improvement in published accounts might be obtained by the
general adoption of the flow of funds statement in addition to the
existing accounts. The main value of this statement is that it gives
a clear account of the way in which a company is financed, especially
if set out as a series of financial flows for five or more years. It is
relatively simple in form, it draws attention to the changes which have
taken place and it is not materially affected by value judgements.
It provides an additional dimension to the financial picture when added
to the balance sheet and profit and loss account.

*10.4 Efficiency of Management*

Although the degree of control by shareholders is often small, one
might expect that the accounts would provide material to make an
appraisal of efficiency as a spur to questioning by shareholders and as
a guide to investors. In fact it is doubtful whether this service is
performed very well. Accounting statements deal with short term
results, with realised gains and losses, and throw little light on the
condition of the company to produce results in the long term. This is

7. Report of the Tribunal appointed to enquire into certain issues in relation
to the circumstances leading up to the cessation of trading by the
Vehicle and General Insurance Company Limited (1972). H.M.S.O.
HL 80, HC 133.

a fundamental weakness of historic statements which it is suggested is not likely to be overcome. As the longer term view is an important ingredient in the appraisal of current results, financial accounts on their own can only make a limited contribution to the assessment of efficiency. The contribution which they can make depends on the ability to compare results with an appropriate standard of achievement, which will usually mean the achievement of similar companies, and this implies a high degree of comparability of figures. Published accounts are weak in two respects;

1.   in the lack of disclosure in the profit and loss account and
2.   in the lack of comparability of the figures which are disclosed.

The lack of comparability is made more acute when a company operates in several different trades and fails to analyse the contribution of each trade. Steps are being taken to improve accounts in these respects and the work of the Accounting Standards Steering Committee has already been discussed in Chapter 6.

One might argue that, apart from the contents of the profit and loss account, we are near the limits of the amount of detail which should be disclosed and that already the accounts are too complicated for the ordinary informed reader as distinct from the expert analyst. If the shareholder is to be informed directly, through the annual report, of the company's financial affairs it is not sufficient to present him with a mass of historical data on which he must spend a lot of time if he wishes to learn anything from it. What he needs is a relatively simple report which analyses the financial situation and the results and highlights the important aspects. In order to do this such a report must provide the standards against which the results produced by the company are to be judged and an explanation of material differences. This implies a statement which contains the more important ratios, comparisons with other companies in the industry and trends of the main figures. Although many companies do provide a summary of the main figures in the accounts for a period of several years there is no attempt generally to provide the shareholder with a report based on a critical examination of the figures. It is possible that many companies do not make such an appraisal for their own benefit and might gain from having to do it for the shareholders. Such a report, being based on historical figures should be capable of audit at least in so far as the accuracy of the figures is concerned, and the full accounts would provide the specialist with any other information which he required.

## 10.5 Investment Decisions

Financial information is useful in the decision to buy or sell shares to the extent that it improves the estimates of the underlying values of shares. In theory one needs a reliable estimate of the future trend of dividends over a long period of time together with a measure of the risk involved in the investment and the trend of interest rates. In other words the information which is required relates to the future and is largely outside the scope of historical financial statements, however much they are improved. The present position is the point from which estimates must start and past results will act as a test of the reasonableness or otherwise of any forecasts which are made, but this is a limited contribution. It seems unlikely that we will attain the state when the value of the company can be reflected in the report of the current position, even if it were theoretically possible. The use of current values in the balance sheet, though desirable, will not bring this about because the use of such values must normally be confined to tangible assets such as building and plant.[8]

The direct contribution which is made by the financial accounts is to provide an up to date statement of the current position as a basis for forecasting. The type of business and assets held by the company, the cash resources, the present management, the financial structure all constrain the development which can be expected. If substantial changes in position and profitability take place, they may have a material effect on future potential and therefore on the value of the shares. The incomplete nature of our expectations for the future is reflected in the emphasis which is given to the prompt reporting of financial results and all events which are likely to have a material effect on share values. The importance of up to date

8. Suggestions have been made for incorporating in the balance sheet the value of people employed by the company but we lack convincing evidence that this is either reasonable or appropriate.

information is recognised in the Stock Exchange requirement that half yearly reports shall be issued and the suggestion of the English and Scottish Institutes of Chartered Accountants that legislation should enforce publication of accounts within 6 months of the financial year end (or 9 months if the company has overseas interests). It is also recognised that companies must avoid the possibility that privileged individuals may be able to use advance knowledge to deal advantageously at the expense of other investors. The Memorandum of Guidance on Communication of Announcements issued by the Stock Exchange suggests that information should be communicated by the company direct to the Stock Exchange to prevent information reaching the market after it has been communicated elsewhere. Directors of companies are normally aware of events before shareholders, but the provisions of the Companies Acts requiring publication of directors' shareholdings exercise a constraint on the use of such information. The problem of dealings in shares by 'insiders' with private knowledge, is however, an important one and is likely to receive increased attention.

Nevertheless, whilst it is important that investors receive a clear account of the current situation promptly at regular intervals and that any major changes which materially affect the status of the investment are reported widely as they occur, it is a mistake to expect too much of the historical statements. Their contribution to the investment decision is an indirect one. They are the start of the analysis not the final product.

If statements are to be developed for the purpose of giving more specific guidance to shareholders in their decisions it will be necessary to allow some insight into the plans of management for some years ahead. One step which has been widely advocated is the reporting of budgets for the next 12 months. Whilst this would add to our knowledge of companies the advantage may not in fact very be great. In the first place the provision of a budget for 12 months in advance is only a small step in the valuation procedure; it is still a very short term view and one which suffers from most of the defects of the historical accounts. As a test of liquidity, particularly in ensuring that directors make a serious examination of the cash position, it would be valuable. As a basis for forecasting profitability it would be suspect because of the ability to adjust short term results at the expense of long term welfare of the company. Even as a test of efficiency of management the comparison of actual results with budget presents problems unless a detailed report with explanations is to be given.

Secondly, doubt has been expressed as to the ability of many companies to provide reasonably accurate figures for several months ahead. As an example, a review of forecasts made in takeover bid situations suggested that only 50% of profit forecasts made 10 months before the end of the accounting year or earlier are likely to be within 10% of the actual result and that there tended to be a pessimistic bias in the forecasts.[9] The results revealed by this survey may be affected by the fact that the forecasts were made in bid situations, in some cases at short notice, and that actual results of firms taken over may have been affected by the change in management. A regular forecast by an established management might be expected to provide a better indication of the final outcome. On the other hand a review of internal budgets in a small sample of companies in the United States did not suggest a high degree of accuracy in forecasting net profit— differences exceeding 15% between forecasted and actual profit were observed in one-third of the 65 observations. Forecasts of sales were much better but forecasted balance sheet data could not be studied because companies either did not produce it or regarded it as very inaccurate.[10]

If a sound basis is to be laid for valuation then it would appear to be necessary to publish an outline of the planned development of the company over a period of several years. If the plans are to be capable of critical appraisal it would be necessary to make explicit the assumptions on which the plans were based, including the general economic and political background to the company's planning. If the material were meant for the information of the ordinary shareholder, it would need to be presented in a concise report and would require the support of an independent analyst, as well as the authority of the directors. It is perhaps not too fanciful to anticipate

9. WESTWICK, C A, Profit Forecasts in Bid Situations, *Accountancy*, July 1972, pp. 10–16.
10. DAILY, R A, The Feasibility of Reporting Forecasted Information, *Accounting Review*, October 1971, pp. 686–92.

the possibility that companies should apply such an analysis of their prospects on an annual basis. A well managed company should have the material to do so and could ensure wide dissemination of the information. On the other hand there are cogent arguments against the practice. The forecasts must depend on plans of the existing board and would not normally anticipate the effects of a takeover bid or change in management; there may be sound commercial reasons why new developments should not be published until results have been achieved; there are doubts as to the ability of many companies to provide such analysis; the problems of defining responsibility and of audit are very great.

In the absence of such analysis, made on a recurring basis, one has little information about the long term progress of a company. The short term reports provided by the traditional accounts are not a good basis for judging plans which will not mature for many years. On the other hand there is need for much more knowledge of the possibility of providing reasonable forecasts and the effects of requiring such forecasts before a case could be made for compelling companies to produce them. We can say that if financial information is to be designed to provide a basis for investors' decisions then attention must be given primarily to forecasting rather than to historical accounts. What we can not say is that we are ready to take such a big step forward.

*10.6 Summary*

The accounts which are published at the present perform a useful function in compelling directors to account for the use of the funds placed at the disposal of the company, in directing attention to the financial position and providing data which may be used in analysing solvency. They are less effective for analysing the efficiency of management. There is no doubt that published accounts can be improved but it is suggested that the amount of detail which is provided is already near the limit and that, for the ordinary shareholder at least, other methods are needed. One improvement for the shareholder would be the provision of a short critical examination of the results and position of the company.

Accounts contribute to the knowledge required for investment decisions but they cannot provide the sort of information which is needed directly. Accounts are history whereas valuation needs forecasts. If annual reports are to be designed to give more guidance to the investor, thought should be given to the provision of forecast data rather than attempting to place too much burden on the historical documents.

There is no limit to the information which could be supplied by a company except that which is imposed by time and cost. In practice there is a tendency to measure what can be easily measured, to report what can be easily provided. No attempt is made to measure potential benefit to investors of different types of information or the cost of supplying other information. In the case of the historic accounts which are produced it seems reasonable to assume that the benefits substantially exceed the costs. The accounts are fairly easy to produce from existing records, and serve several purposes including use by management and tax authorities as well as investors. Relatively minor changes such as more disclosure in the profit and loss account can be recommended with confidence that the cost is minimal and the gain in information is substantial. Similarly the publication of a concise analysis of the past figures is much easier for the company to produce than for shareholders to do individually and without it the accounts lose much of their value. The question whether forecast information should be provided is not so obviously answered in the affirmative. It is suggested that until we have at least some crude estimates of costs and benefits we are not on very firm ground in recommending this extension to annual reports.

# Appendix

*A summary of the information which must be reported in published accounts and the directors' report to comply with the Companies Acts*

The *summary* is designed to identify in detail the minimum information which the reader can expect to find in all published accounts. References are to paragraphs of the Companies Act 1967 Schedule 2 unless otherwise indicated. Other references show the Act and section number, thus: (1948 s. 148) refers to the Companies Act 1948 section 148. Minor amendments have been made by Companies (Accounts) Regulations 1970 and 1971. There are exemptions from a number of the requirements in the case of banking, insurance and shipping companies (see 1967, Schedule 2, part III) and in other cases with the consent of the Department of Trade and Industry. Additions to the legal requirements listed here have been made by the Statements of Standard Accounting Practice and, for some companies, by the requirements of the Stock Exchange, discussed in chapter 6.

    *The Balance Sheet and Profit and Loss Account*—to be published not later than eighteen months after incorporation and subsequently at least once in every calender year; to be made up to a date not earlier than nine months[1] before the date of the meeting at which they are presented (1948, s. 148). The balance sheet is to give a true and fair view of the state of affairs as at the end of the financial year and the

1. Twelve months in the case of a company having interests abroad.

profit and loss account a true and fair view of the profit or loss for the year (1948, s. 149). The auditors' report is to be attached to the balance sheet (1948, s. 156).

*Group Accounts.* A holding company (a company with subsidiaries)[2] must produce, in addition to its own accounts, group accounts which are normally to be in the form of a consolidated balance sheet and profit and loss account (1948, s. 150, 151).

If a consolidated profit and loss account is produced the company's own profit and loss account may be dispensed with, but there must be shown the amount of profit or loss of the holding company in addition to the profit or loss of the group.

There are a number of exemptions from the requirement to produce group accounts, including the fact that the holding company is the wholly owned subsidiary of another company, but if group accounts are not submitted, the reasons for not dealing with subsidiaries in group accounts and information relating to profits and qualifications in auditors' reports on subsidiaries must be given (15(4) and 1948, s. 150).

A holding company's directors are to secure that the financial year of each subsidiary coincides with that of the holding company, unless there are good reasons against it (1948, s. 153). If the years do not coincide a statement of the reasons and the dates of the subsidiaries' financial years is required (15 and 22).

The information to be disclosed in the accounts applies to the consolidated accounts as if they were the accounts of an actual company except that:

1.  the disclosure of directors' emoluments, loans to officers and remuneration of employees earning more than £10,000 per annum applies only in respect of the holding company's directors and senior employees.

2.  the provisions dealing with the disclosure of holdings exceeding 10% of the equity of another company, or exceeding 10% of the assets of the holding company do not apply to the group accounts (19).

2. Defined in chapter 4.2.

*A subsidiary company* must state the name of the body corporate regarded by the directors as being its ultimate holding company and the country in which it is incorporated (1967, s. 5).

CONTENTS OF THE BALANCE SHEET

Share capital

—A summary of authorised and issued capital. (2) Authorised capital is the maximum nominal amount which the company may issue. The amount may be altered from time to time in accordance with the regulations of the company. Issued capital is the nominal amount of shares allotted to members.

—Redeemable preference shares: the earliest and latest dates of redemption; whether redemption is compulsory or at the option of the company; and the premium payable if any (2a).

—Share capital on which interest has been paid out of capital during the financial year and the rate at which paid (2b). The right to pay such interest is subject to the sanction of the Department of Trade and Industry.

—Premium on shares: the excess over the nominal amount received in respect of shares issued must be stated separately, and is usually classified with reserves (2c).

—Options on shares showing the number, description and amount, the period during which each option is exercisable and the price to be paid for the shares (11).

—In the case of a holding company if any of its shares are held by a subsidiary company (other than as trustee or as security for a loan made in the ordinary course of business) there must be a note of the number, description and amount of the shares held (15). It has not been possible to acquire additional shares in this category since 1948 (1948, s. 27).

Reserves

—The aggregate amount, classified under appropriate headings, and giving an account of changes during the financial period (4, 6 and 7).

Liabilities

—Summarised and indicating their general nature (2) and

classified under headings appropriate to the company's business
(4).

—The aggregate amount of bank loans and overdrafts (8).

—The aggregate amount of other loans which fall due for
repayment more than 5 years after the balance sheet date
(including loans repayable by instalments where the repayment
period exceeds 5 years), the terms of repayment and rate of
interest (8).

—The recommended dividend (8).

—Arrears of fixed cumulative preference dividends, stating for
each class the amount and the period for which in arrear (11).

—If a liability is secured on any assets of the company the fact
that it is secured. The assets need not be identified (9).

—Particulars of any charge on assets to secure the liabilities of
another person including the amount secured if practicable (11).

—The aggregate amount of provisions and an account of changes
during the financial period. In this context a provision is a
known liability of which the amount cannot be determined with
substantial accuracy (6, 7 and 27).

—The general nature of any contingent liabilities not provided
for and the amount if practicable (11).

—The aggregate amount of contracts for capital expenditure not
provided for (11).

—The aggregate amount of capital expenditure authorised by the
directors but not yet contracted for (11).

—The aggregate amount of indebtedness to subsidiary companies
(15).

—The aggregate amount of indebtedness to holding companies
and fellow subsidiaries (16).

## Debentures

—If a company has redeemed debentures and has power to
re-issue them particulars must be stated. If the company has
purchased its own debentures and holds them as an asset the
nominal amount held and the amount at which they are stated
in the books must be stated (10). (A debenture is a loan stock
and may be either secured or unsecured.) If a subsidiary

company holds debentures in the holding company, the holding company must state the description and amount of the debentures held, unless they are held as trustee or as security for a loan made in the ordinary course of business.

Taxation
—The basis on which the amount set aside for United Kingdom corporation tax is computed (11).
—The amount, if any, set aside for the purpose of its being used to prevent undue fluctuations in charges for taxation (often referred to as deferred taxation) (7A). If the amount set aside is used for any other purpose details must be given (11).

Foreign currencies
—The basis of conversion into sterling (11).

Assets
—Summarised, classified under headings appropriate to the company's business and disclosing their general nature. Fixed assets, current assets and assets which are neither fixed nor current must be separately identified (2, 4).

Fixed assets
—The method used to calculate the amount of each category (4). The normal method is to state either the cost or valuation, the aggregate depreciation since acquisition or valuation, and the net amount remaining (5). If assets are stated at a valuation, the years in which the valuations were made, and for a valuation in the current financial year, the names or qualifications of the valuers and the basis of valuation must be stated (11). Exceptions to the normal method apply in respect of investments in subsidiary companies, other investments for which the current value is shown, goodwill patents and trademarks, and assets the replacement of which is charged direct to profit and loss account or to a provision for replacement. If this replacement basis is used, the means of providing for replacement and the balance of any provision for renewal must be given (5).

—The aggregate amount of each category (other than investments) acquired and disposed of during the financial year (11).
—Separately, freehold land, land held on long lease (at least 50 years unexpired) and land held on short lease (11).

Investments (other than in subsidiary companies)
—The aggregate amounts of the quoted investments and of the unquoted investments (8). A quoted investment is one for which a quotation or permission to deal has been granted on a recognised stock exchange or on any stock exchange of repute outside Great Britain (28).
—If the company holds equity shares comprising more than one-tenth of the nominal value of the issued shares of that class there must be stated (1) the name of the company, the shares of which are held, and the place of incorporation, (2) the class of shares and the proportion held, (3) particulars of any other shares held in the same company.
—If the company holds shares in another company and the amount stated in the accounts as an asset exceeds one-tenth of the total assets of the investing company the information stated in (1) and (2) above must be given (1967, s. 4).

Quoted investments
—The market value, and if this is greater than the stock exchange value, the stock exchange value. The value may be shown as the balance sheet value or by way of note (11).

Unquoted investments
—Either (a) the cost or valuation and accumulated depreciation as in the normal method for fixed assets, or (b) in the case of current assets, the cost or lower realisable value, or (c) the value at the date of the balance sheet estimated by the directors.
—In the case of equity shares, the current value of which is not shown, there must also be stated (i) the amount of the current year's income ascribable to the investments, (ii) the company's share of profits less losses, both before and after tax, of the companies in which shares are held, (iii) the company's share

of the undistributed profits of those companies, accumulated since the shares were acquired, (iv) the manner in which any losses incurred by those companies have been dealt with in the investing company's accounts (5A).

Investment in subsidiary companies
  —The aggregate amount of shares in subsidiaries.
  —The aggregate amount owing to the holding company by subsidiaries.
  —The aggregate amount of indebtedness to subsidiaries (15).
  —A note or statement showing, for each subsidiary, its name, whether registered in England or Scotland or if incorporated abroad the country of incorporation, and the proportion of the nominal value of each class of shares held. The statement may be restricted to subsidiaries which principally affect the profit or amount of assets of the group if it would otherwise be of excessive length (1967, s. 3).

Investments in holding companies and fellow subsidiaries
  —The aggregate indebtedness of those companies distinguishing debentures and other indebtedness.
  —The aggregate amount of shares in fellow subsidiaries. Companies are fellow subsidiaries if they are both subsidiaries of the same holding company but neither is the subsidiary of the other (16).

Intangible assets
  —Goodwill, patents and trade marks must be stated as a separate item in so far as the cost has not been written off (8).
  —A number of expenses are sometimes carried forward instead of being written off to profit and loss account when incurred and so appear as assets in the balance sheet. The following must be separately stated (a) preliminary expenses of forming the company, (b) expenses of issue of share capital or debentures, (c) commission paid in respect of shares or debentures, (d) discount allowed in respect of debentures, (e) discount allowed on any issue of shares (3).

Current assets
—If the amount carried forward for stock in trade or work in
progress is material for the appreciation of the position or
profit, the manner in which the amount has been computed (11).
—If in the opinion of the directors any of the current assets are
stated at a value in excess of that which is expected to be
realisable in the ordinary course of trade they must state so (11).

Loans to officers of the company
—The amount of loans made and repaid during the year and the
amount outstanding at the end of the year. This includes
amounts lent by subsidiary companies and by others under
guarantee or on security provided by the company or its
subsidiaries but excludes loans made in the ordinary course of
business of the company or its subsidiaries (1948, s. 197).
—Loans to employees or to trustees for employees to acquire
shares in the company or its holding company in accordance
with 1948, s. 54 (1b and c). The aggregate amount outstanding
is to be shown (8).

Comparative figures
—For the previous year except in the case of details of the changes
in fixed assets and movements in reserves (11).

CONTENTS OF THE PROFIT AND LOSS ACCOUNT

There must be stated:

The amount of any charge or credit arising from an event in a
preceding financial year (12A).

The effect of transactions of a sort not usually undertaken by the
company, or of an exceptional or non-recurrent nature (14).

The effect of any change in the basis of accounting (14).

Comparative figures for the previous year (14 and 1967, s. 11).

The following detailed information:

*Revenue :*
Turnover
—Not being defined it is left to the directors to state the figure
   which they believe provides the best indication. In general it
   represents the amount receivable for goods sold by the company
   as a principal or for services rendered in the ordinary course of
   business. It does not include the sale of capital assets such as
   buildings or plant. Companies with turnover up to £250,000
   are exempt from disclosing turnover. The method of calculating
   turnover should be stated (13A).

Rents from land and buildings
—If a substantial part of the company's revenue is derived from
   rents the net amount after deducting ground rents, rates and
   other outgoings are to be shown (12).

Income from quoted investments (12)
Income from unquoted investments (12)

*Expenses and appropriation of profit :*
Depreciation
—The provision for depreciation, renewals or diminution in value
   of fixed assets. If the charge for depreciation or diminution in
   value is not determined by reference to the amount of the assets
   in the balance sheet (if it is not a conventional depreciation
   charge) (12) or if no provision is made for depreciation or
   renewal (14) this must be stated.
—A provision for renewal, made in addition to the charge for
   depreciation is to be shown separately (12).

Provisions
—Amounts set aside for, or withdrawn from provisions other than
   depreciation, etc., mentioned above (12).

Interest
—In two categories. (*i*) Payable on bank loans and overdrafts
   and on loans which are wholly repayable within 5 years of the
   date of the balance sheet, (*ii*) payable on other loans (12).

Auditors' remuneration
—Including expenses (13).

Directors' emoluments
—The aggregate of the emoluments of the directors of the company
for service to the company and its subsidiary companies,
whether payable by the company, the subsidiary or anyone
else and distinguishing emoluments for services as director and
other emoluments.
—The aggregate amount of directors' or past directors' pensions,
other than pensions under a pension scheme for which
contributions are adequate to maintain the scheme. Pensions
are to be divided between those for services as director and
other pensions.
—The aggregate compensation to directors or past directors for
loss of office similarly divided.
—The emoluments of the chairman.
—An analysis of the number of directors whose emoluments were
not more than £2,500, the number over £2,500 up to £5,000
and in each successive class of similar size. Exemption is granted
for directors whose duties are mainly abroad.
—If the emoluments of the highest paid director (other than a
director whose duties are mainly abroad) exceed those of the
chairman, then his emoluments must be stated separately.
—If directors have waived rights to receive emoluments for the
period the number of directors and the aggregate amount
waived.
—There are exemptions for companies which are neither holding
nor subsidiary companies where the aggregate emoluments
shown in the accounts do not exceed £15,000 (1948, s. 196
and 1967, s. 6 and 7).

Emoluments of employees
—An analysis of the number of employees earning more than
£10,000 per annum, in classes with a range of £2,500 (as in
the case of directors). Total wages for all employees must be
stated in the directors' report (1967, s. 8).

Expense of hire of plant and machinery (12)

United Kingdom corporation tax
—If reduced by relief for foreign tax, the gross amount before such relief, the actual UK tax and foreign tax (12).
—The basis of the charge for UK corporation tax and income tax (14).
—Special circumstances affecting the liability for tax for the current or succeeding years (14).

Dividends
—The aggregate amount (before deduction of income tax) of the dividends paid and proposed (12).

Reserves
—Amounts set aside or withdrawn from reserves.
—Amounts set aside for redemption of share capital and loans (12).

THE REPORT OF THE DIRECTORS (1948, s. 157 and 1967, s. 15–22)
The Companies Acts require a report of the directors to be attached to every balance sheet with respect to the state of the company's affairs, the principal activities of the company and its subsidiaries and any significant changes in those activities during the year. The following details are specified:

Fixed assets
—Particulars of significant changes during the year in the fixed assets of the company and its subsidiaries.
—The difference between the market value of land and buildings and the amount stated in the balance sheet if in the opinion of the directors it is of such significance as to require attention to be drawn to it.

Shares and debentures
—If a new issue has been made during the year, the reason for the issue, the classes issued and the number in each class and the consideration received.

Directors' interests

—The names of the directors of the company.

—Particulars of contracts with the company, other than his contract of service, in which a director had an interest at any time in the year, if significant. (This does not appear to include contracts with a subsidiary company.)

—Details of schemes for directors to acquire benefits by the acquisition of shares or debentures in the company, or any other body corporate.

—Details of shares and debentures held by or in trust for a director or any right to acquire such holdings, including shares or debentures in the company's holding or subsidiary companies.

Classes of business

—If the company (or group of companies) carries on two or more classes of business which in the opinion of the directors differ substantially from each other: (a) the proportion of turnover in each class, (b) the amount which each class contributed to the profit or loss for the year (before taxation).

Employees

—The average number of persons employed by the company or group and the aggregate remuneration for the year. Persons who are employed wholly or mainly outside the United Kingdom are excluded and the information need not be given if the average number is less than 100.

Gifts

—Details of money given for political and charitable purposes if the total amount given by the company or group in the year exceeds £50.

Exports

—A statement of the aggregate value of goods exported from the UK in the year, unless the company or group is exempt from showing turnover or does not supply goods.

Other matters
  —Any matters which are material for the appreciation of the state
  of the company's affairs by its members, unless in the opinion
  of the directors disclosure would be harmful to the business.

# Index